GHOSTS

GHOSTS
True Stories from British Columbia

Robert C. Belyk

HORSDAL & SCHUBART

Horsdal & Schubart Publishers Ltd.
Victoria, BC

Cover art and line drawings by Suzanne Gagnon, Ganges, BC.

Design and typesetting by The Typeworks, Vancouver, BC. This book is set in Walbaum. Printed and bound in Canada by Hignell Printing Limited, Winnipeg, Manitoba.

This book is for Margaret.

Canadian Cataloguing in Publication Data
    Belyk, Robert C., 1944-
    Ghosts
    Includes bibliographical references.
    ISBN 0-920663-09-5
    1. Ghosts--British Columbia.   I. Title.
    BF1472.C2B44   1990   133.1'09711   C90-091458-0

Contents

PART IV: Early British Columbia Ghost Stories

Preface

Several years ago the provincial Ministry of Tourism launched an advertising campaign using the slogan, "Super, Natural British Columbia." They were, of course, not referring to weird or bizarre happenings in the province. This was simply a play on words, drawing attention to the province's truly magnificent scenery. Yet there is a strange irony here: the slogan is also quite correct, for without doubt, British Columbia is one of Canada's most haunted provinces.

This book is a collection of some of the most interesting British Columbia ghost stories from the past and the present. These accounts have been taken from diverse sources, including British Columbia archive files and newspaper accounts, as well as first-hand interviews. Although very different in content, these stories have one element in common: they are all claimed by their sources to be true.

Although I have included quite a few tales in this work, I realize this does not begin to scratch the surface of this province's ghost lore. If you have further information concerning any of the stories included here, or have had other ghostly encounters in British Columbia, I would like to hear from you. Please write me care of the publisher:

Horsdal & Schubart Publishers Ltd.
Post Office Box 1
Ganges, British Columbia
Canada VOS 1EO

Robert C. Belyk

Introduction: About Ghosts and Ghost Stories

This book is about British Columbia ghosts. Although the stories presented here are limited geographically to one region, they are as diverse a collection of ghost stories as one can imagine. Unlike fictional ghost tales, which can be counted on to relieve the reader's building tension by the final page, actual stories of the supernatural are always a little unsatisfying. These stories have an unpolished feel to them; the pieces do not seem to fit together. Often, important questions are not answered. The reader is left to scratch his or her head and wonder.

Yet there is another side to this equation. These ghost stories are about real people — actual accounts of men and women who have come face to face with the world of the preternatural. For some of us, ghost stories offer nothing more than an exciting read. For others, however, these accounts point toward something more. They are a definite break with a reality that seems, on the surface at least, very well understood. These stories are a disturbing prick at our day-to-day existence — a tangible reminder that the world is a good deal more complicated than we care to acknowledge.

Ghost stories are open to widely varying interpretations. Until quite recently, the study of ghosts has been of interest only to those delving into the field of the occult. However, in 1882, a number of prominent British academics moved toward applying the tools of science to the study of ghosts. The organization they founded was known as the Society for Psychical Research

(SPR). The SPR has served as a model for psychic research throughout the world.

So Many Ghosts

Those interested in Canadian ghostlore will be impressed by the sheer volume of British Columbia ghost tales. There are few such ghost tales on the prairies (although Alberta seems to have more than the other two provinces) and only a small number in Quebec. Ontario has quite a rich collection of ghost stories, but with its far greater population, one would expect that there would be many more incidents there than in British Columbia, and this is not the case. In relation to population, only the Maritime region, with its long history of phantom ships, ghostly crews and the like, clearly has more ghost stories than British Columbia.

Interestingly, there are several theories that may account for British Columbia's large population of ghosts. First, there is the climate theory. The idea that climate plays a role in the frequency of psychic manifestations has been around for a number of years as folk knowledge. In 1963, however, the notion was given serious consideration by the distinguished anthropologist Margaret Murray, who wrote, "As [the ghost phenomenon] is known to occur in many parts of the world, it is worth noting that it is more common in moist climates than drier ones."[1] Thus, she concluded, apparitions are seen more frequently in the moister regions of Scotland and Ireland than in England with its drier climate, and similarly, the monsoon regions of India have more ghosts than the desert areas of Egypt. Like the image on a frame of photographic film, Dr. Murray believed, ghosts required the right chemical conditions to manifest themselves, and the correct conditions were somehow associated with a wet or humid atmosphere.

At first glance, British Columbia's pattern of ghostly activity seems to fit Dr. Murray's theory. If the number of ghost stories in the Provincial Archives will serve as a rough indicator of a region's "hauntedness," then the wet coast is far more haunted than the much drier interior. Yet there are other factors that need to be taken into account. It is also true that the most densely populated regions of the province — places where, statistically, one would expect to have more incidents reported — are also along the coast. Moreover, at least one dry area seems to have more than its share of ghosts — the old mining town of Barkerville in the Cariboo district. Thus, as far as British Columbia is concerned, it is difficult to draw any positive conclusions about the relationship between ghosts and climate.

There is a second theory — this one proposed by the psychic researcher T.C. Lethbridge — that may be more promising. Some time in the 1950s, while Mr. Lethbridge and his wife were walking along the English coast, they passed near a small stream which ran down from the cliffs nearby. Suddenly, for no apparent reason, he was overcome by a profound feeling of depression. As Lethbridge moved away from the swift-running water the feeling of despondency lifted as abruptly as it had descended upon him. He mentioned the experience to his wife, Mina, who told him she had experienced the same changes in mood.

Later that day Mrs. Lethbridge was again overcome by a feeling of severe melancholy. She had walked up the trail to the top of the cliff where she planned to sketch the scene before her. The best spot was near a stream which eventually tumbled over the cliff to the beach below, the same stream which had so badly affected both Lethbridges earlier. She had not been working on her picture long before she was aware of a strong impulse to throw herself from the heights. Not surprisingly, Mrs. Lethbridge was very distressed by the feeling.

The couple later discovered that a man had thrown himself from the cliff — at the exact spot where Mrs. Lethbridge was sketching. The incident led Lethbridge to consider whether it was possible that the energy field generated by the moving water could somehow record psychic impressions. Certain events, he later argued, would be impressed on the water's field of energy in much the same way that sound is impressed on the magnetic field of a reel of tape.

The idea that objects "record" human events which are later "played back" to a "receiver" (a person sensitive to psychic vibrations) was not a new one. As early as 1885, Mrs. Eleanor Sidgwick, one of the pioneer members of Britain's Society for Psychical Research, postulated that apparitions were the result of something that was physically part of the structure. However, the notion that psychic impressions were associated with bodies of water was revolutionary.

Like the climate theory, Lethbridge's water-field theory appears initially quite plausible. The problem is that with the west coast's high annual rainfall, it is difficult to find any location where water is not close at hand, and the question may thus become not why there are so many ghosts, but why there are not more.

Two Kinds Of Hauntings

For many years now psychic researchers have tried to come to terms with what makes one haunting case similar to or different from another, and what they have determined is that there are indeed two major kinds of ghosts: *those that haunt places* and *those that haunt people.*

The first category of ghosts is the place-haunting variety. Houses account for the greatest percentage of reported hauntings, but ghosts, it seems, can haunt just about anything — from elevators to submarines. There is a particularly well-documented case of a haunted German U-boat during the First World War. Place-haunting ghosts can occupy one spot for decades, or even centuries. If all the legends are to be believed, ghosts of historical figures like Queen Mary of Scotland and Sir Walter Raleigh continue to haunt Britain's old castles.

In many instances the haunting consists of very simple acts — the sound of footsteps in the hall, for example — which are repeated over and over. Often those living in haunted houses begin to take these occurrences for granted: the strange inci-

4

dents become routine rather than frightening.

While the sound of phantom footsteps is one common form of this ghostly phenomenon, spectral sightings are fairly unusual. Rarer still is speech — place-haunting ghosts seldom talk to anyone (any living person at least). Since ghosts do not have vocal cords, psychic researchers speculate that speech simulation takes a considerable amount of a ghost's energy. Ghosts have been known to try to speak, but often they succeed only in mouthing the words; very rarely is speech actually heard. (Incidentally, the result of a ghost's use of energy may be "cold spots"— areas with drops in temperature that are frequently noted during hauntings.)

On some occasions smells are associated with a haunting. Usually these odours are pleasant, but this is not always the case. For example, 20 years ago there was a case of an odour haunting of the landlord of a pub in Huntingdonshire, England. Whenever the man entered the old section of his pub a singularly unpleasant smell clung to him, leaving only when he returned to the new addition. The odour was very repugnant, reminding those who experienced it of a decaying carcass.

In some cases the psychic experience reported by witnesses goes beyond the perception of ghostly images, smells or sounds. In these instances it is as though a hole in the fabric of time is opened — that one "sees" directly into the past. For example, a person may visit an old castle and say that he has seen the ghost of a former resident: a duke who died in 1590. When the individual is questioned it becomes clear that the incident involves more than just an ordinary haunting: the person saw not only the ghost of the 16th-century duke, but also the castle as it stood at that time. If he happened to look out a castle window, the countryside would appear not as today, but as it was four hundred years ago.

"Retrocognition," as this phenomenon is termed, is fairly common in psychical literature. One of the best-known recent examples took place in 1951 at a place not far from the beach at Dieppe, France. Two English women who were spending their summer vacation at a small hotel on the coast of France were awakened early in the morning by the sounds of airplanes, gunfire, and the cries of men. The noise of battle continued for about two hours before finally fading away.

While there were other people staying at the hotel, the two women were the only witnesses and as far as they were concerned there was no question as to the sounds rising up from the beach. (They had even ventured out on the balcony of their room so they could hear better.) The hotel was located near where the infamous Dieppe Raid occurred in 1942. There, during an abortive World War II landing, many hundreds of Canadian soldiers met their deaths. What the two women believed they heard was the sound of that ill-fated wartime operation which had taken place nine years earlier.

Not all ghosts can be associated with the notion of either recordings or retrocognition. In many cases it seems clear that the ghostly activity is not simply a playback of the past: there is some form of intelligence behind a haunting. Indeed, often the actions of place-haunting ghosts are so purposeful they can best be described as mischievous. Their actions are usually very simple and repetitive: unscrewing some of the lights on a Christmas tree was a favourite activity of one particular ghost; turning on a tea kettle was another. For the psychic investigator, what is obvious about these ghosts is that their "tricks" seem to lack sophistication. Witnesses often describe this behaviour as child-like and some researchers speculate that it may be attention-seeking. What the ghost is really trying to say is, "Hey, notice me. I'm here too!"

The people-haunting variety — where the individual is haunted by his own particular spirit — is by far the smallest category of ghostly manifestation. There are stories of individuals being followed everywhere by mysterious shadows or even sounds — a Victoria newspaper editor, David W. Higgins, once wrote about a local man who was plagued by the sound of footsteps. Overall though, this kind of personal ghost seems quite rare.

A more ubiquitous personal ghost is the type which is commonly termed "crisis apparition." Crisis apparitions are different from most types of ghosts in that they may be spirits of the living rather than the dead. By definition, their appearance is always associated with intense personal crisis (and this almost inevitably involves death). A typical example of a crisis apparition would be a terminally ill patient appearing to a friend or relative (often miles away) one or two days *before* death. While in some cases the crisis apparition is seen after the person's death, it is never long afterwards, usually within 12 hours. The appearance of these ghosts is frequently associated with the delivery of a final personal message (either explicit or implied) to friends or loved ones. After the single visit, the apparition is usually never seen again.

A particularly nasty category of people-haunting ghost is the poltergeist. The term *poltergeist* means, in German, "noisy ghost", and, true to its name, the poltergeist is known for breaking cups, plates, and glasses, tossing furniture about and creating a considerable fuss. For those unfortunate enough to be the focus of its malicious activities the haunting can be very physical — individuals have been pelted with stones, or unceremoniously tossed from a bed onto the floor. (Rarely, though, is anyone hurt by the actions of the poltergeist.) Although modern parapsychology has come some way in understanding poltergeist activity, exactly what they are, and why they haunt some individuals and not others, is still a mystery.

The Old And The New

The reader who is unfamiliar with ghost stories of the non-fiction variety will find that these tales are rather an odd collection. Ghosts are a mixed lot. They come in just about every shape and size, and do just about anything one can imagine. This makes the organization of the material somewhat difficult, but there are several logical approaches to the subject.

For one thing, there is a definite difference between old and new British Columbia ghost stories. Many (but by no means all) of the tales from before the First World War fall into the folk-narrative category — a story told and retold for generations. Often what happens is that eventually, some enterprising journalist hears the tale and realizes it will make a great story. The reporter then files this worn account as if it were current news. Of course, as one might imagine, the folk narrative tends to be less accurate than other ghost stories reported first or even second hand.

About the time of the First World War there is a change in the way newspapers presented British Columbia ghost stories. After 1918, the accounts tend to be more sophisticated and detailed; there is an increase in interviews with witnesses, and a decrease in folk narratives.

Ghosts And Science

One clear fact that seems to apply to both the place-haunting and people-haunting varieties of ghost is that they are not bound by any known physical laws. Sometimes as wispy as mist, sometimes as solid-looking as flesh and bone, the ghostly substance is quite beyond our understanding. One of the best-documented occurrences of the last century took place in the city of Cheltenham, England, where the apparition of a woman was seen in the home of Captain F.W. Despard. Between 1882 and 1889 the ghost was observed by no less than 17 different people. The figure was so solid that it was mistaken for a living person on at least two different occasions, yet, when Rosina Despard, one of Captain Despard's daughters, attempted to set string traps for the apparition, it was seen to pass freely through them.

In attempting to understand ghost behaviour, it is simply impossible to reach any universal conclusions. "If one looks for reasons," according to the psychic investigator, D. Scott Rogo, "psychical phenomena will soon catapult the seeker into a quagmire. Unlike the inhabitants of our securely physical world (or the domain of our physical sensations) psychical phenomena do not follow the laws of physics or perception conveniently."[2]

Moreover, because they exist almost exclusively in the "field," place-haunting ghosts stand beyond the reach of modern science. Scientists do not have the luxury of bringing them into the laboratory to study them under a microscope. When Britain's Society for Psychical Research was founded, it was believed that the enigma of ghosts and other psychic manifestations would be solved in a matter of a few years.

Today, over a hundred years later, it must be said that while psychical research has offered some insights into the poltergeist, the traditional ghost remains almost as far removed from human understanding as ever. This does not mean that such ghosts do not exist — as will be seen in subsequent chapters, the experiences of so many credible witnesses cannot be easily dismissed — but it may be that the tools of science are entirely unsuitable for probing the nature of the paranormal. Science has aided our understanding of the material world, but there is a wealth of evidence to suggest this is only part of the picture; that there are other realities which remain beyond our comprehension.

PART I: HAUNTED HOUSES

Tod House: The Ghost Who Hated Christmas

The pleasant-looking white bungalow today seems quite ordinary, though it doubtless has lost some of the charm it once had. Years ago it stood far back from the road in a beautiful orchard which extended all the way down to the sea. It is easy to imagine what it would have been like living there in the spring, amid the glory of the pink blossoms. . . .

Of course times change. Now the trees are all gone. Instead, the dwelling stands in the middle of a comfortable block on a quiet street in the Victoria suburb of Oak Bay, and the only hint that the house might be older than its neighbours is that it is built diagonally on the property. This means it takes up more than a normal-size lot; no modern builder would waste so much valuable land. Indeed, by British Columbia standards the house is ancient — well over 130 years old. But that's not all that makes it interesting. Tod House is, or more correctly, was, haunted.

* * * * *

When they purchased Tod House in late 1944, retired Colonel and Mrs. T. C. Evans were highly sceptical of the ghost stories their neighbours told them. According to Oak Bay locals, Tod House was definitely haunted and they would have been well advised never to have moved in. However, as a former military man with a very practical view of the world, Colonel Evans

Tod House. (COURTESY OF BC ARCHIVES)

simply didn't believe in ghosts. Mrs. Evans was also unimpressed by such stories, so the neighbourhood gossip was all but ignored.

However, not long after the colonel and Mrs. Evans moved into their new home they began to change their minds; the Tod House ghost intended to make its presence felt. What emerged during the next seven years was one of the best-documented hauntings in Canadian history.

Colonel and Mrs. Evans hardly had time to unpack their belongings before they were faced with a number of occurrences that defied logical explanation. Objects that were suspended on hooks in the kitchen began rocking on their own. The door leading from the kitchen to a particularly dark and uninviting cellar would not stay shut, even after it was carefully latched. Filing down the slot that held the latch should have solved the problem but it didn't; neither did jamming a chair against the door at night. Often the next morning the chair would be found several feet away from where it had been placed, while to the Evans's frustration, the cellar door would be standing ajar again. (Finally, in order to keep it shut, it was necessary to put an additional bolt on the door.)

Although shaking up the Evans quite badly at first, the presence did not seem really malevolent. The ghost had very definite likes and dislikes. It appeared to be particularly fond of Mrs. Evans's antique rocker. Frequently the rocker, which had been placed in the living room, would be seen to rock on its own. While the ghost seemed to enjoy this activity very much, the couple did not; indeed, the Evans found the rocking very unnerving. Only when the chair was moved into the hall did the rocking finally stop.

The ghost, on the other hand, had a strong dislike of all kinds of hats. Several times the couple would discover that hats which had been placed neatly on the hat rack by the front door had been taken down and scattered like leaves after an autumn storm, all over the hall floor. The Evans would patiently pick up all the hats only to face the same situation again some time later.

Strangely, although it was downstairs where most of the ghostly activity took place, it was in one of the upstairs rooms where the visitation was most strongly felt. The Evans had decided to use a large upstairs room as the master bedroom, but after spending only a couple of nights there, they moved to another bedroom. Neither the colonel nor Mrs. Evans was able to put their finger on what the feeling was like exactly, but there was undoubtedly something strange about that room, and they avoided spending another night there. As they discovered years later, their fears about that room were well-founded.

One night the Evans heard a tremendous crash from an area of grass at the side of the house. When the colonel rushed out to investigate, he found one of the large bedroom windows, still in its frame, lying on the lawn. It had come from what was known as the "eerie room". When Colonel Evans examined the frame he found that it was in excellent condition, with the nails

still in place. It looked as though someone possessing super-
human strength had pushed the window out by its frame, and
sent it crashing to the grass below.

The unusual occurrences which were taking place now almost regularly had piqued the Evans's curiosity. They had no
idea who (or, indeed, *what*) was perpetrating these phenomena
or why it haunted this particular house. In an effort to find
some explanation, Colonel Evans began to dig into the history
of the little house. Built in 1851 by a retired Hudson's Bay
Company trader, John Tod, the house is reputedly the oldest
private residence in western Canada.

Born in Water Leven, Scotland, in 1788, John Tod arrived in
British Columbia (then known as New Caledonia) in 1813.
Tod, it is said, carried only a medical encyclopedia, a book of
poems by Burns and his Bible. It was a difficult life at best, and
the taciturn Scot with the fiery eyes had his share of trouble.
Not noted for his diplomacy, Tod seemed to have difficulty
dealing with Hudson's Bay Company authorities. At one time,
after incurring the wrath of the company's governor, Sir George
Simpson, Tod was sent to isolated Fort McLeod. By the time he
was finally forgiven nine years later, the unfortunate trader had
all but forgotten the English language, speaking instead a mix-
ture of Indian dialects interspersed with a few English words.

While Tod may have lacked tact, he certainly didn't lack
courage. In 1847, when he was Chief Trader at Fort Kamloops,
Tod is said to have held off Chief Nicola and an angry band of
Kamloops Indians by brandishing a large keg of gunpowder.
The old Scot made it clear to the natives that he would blow up
the fort and everyone in it, including himself, rather than sur-
render. Since the Indians, with Tod, were the only ones in the
compound at the time, they decided not to force the issue, and
left peaceably.

Perhaps because of the harshness of a fur trader's life or,
more likely, the quirks of his nature, Tod failed to make a long-
lasting marriage. Before Tod reluctantly left this earth, he had
had a total of seven wives. His first marriage was apparently
very short: not long after the wedding, Tod's young bride,

Catherine Bristowe, returned to England. The names of many of his later wives and the outcomes of his marriages have become somewhat clouded, but it is known that he married a young singer in 1829. In 1834 he is said to have married Lolu, the daughter of a Kamloops area native chief, and subsequently he had three more Indian wives. It was the ghost of one of Tod's native wives who, many believe, came to haunt Tod House.

After his retirement in 1851, Tod was appointed to the Legislative Council by the new governor of Vancouver Island, James Douglas. Tod bought 460 acres from the Hudson's Bay Company and undertook the construction of a house befitting one of the most important men in the little colony of Vancouver Island. While by today's standards the house seems quite modest, over

John Tod. (COURTESY OF BC ARCHIVES)

a century ago it must have turned the eye of many a Vancouver Island pioneer. The most outstanding feature of the dwelling was the fact that it was built of milled lumber rather than rough-hewn logs; the first water-powered sawmill on Vancouver Island had begun operation hardly more than a year earlier. The nails used in the house were hand forged at considerable expense.

The area Tod chose for his new home was then a virtual wilderness, populated only by fur traders and not entirely friendly Indians. Thus for protection, the front door was very thick. (A wise precaution, for the bullet hole in the door attests to the mood of one Cadboro Bay band.) In addition, a tunnel was dug from the mysterious cellar, with the self-opening door, to a spot some distance from the house. The tunnel was to provide Tod, his current wife and ten children, as well as servants, with a means of escape should all else fail.

John Tod lived to be a very old man and, when he finally died in 1882, the house passed to his heirs. There is no record that either Tod or his descendants were haunted by what came to be known as the Tod House ghost, but then, Tod's family could have had good reason to keep the story of the family ghost to themselves. The old trader may have almost literally had a skeleton in his closet.

Meanwhile, Colonel and Mrs. Evans continued to experience the presence. During the first Christmas they occupied the house, the couple spent many hours decorating; on Christmas Eve they were both very tired so they retired to bed early. They apparently slept soundly and heard nothing during the night. When they awoke on Christmas morning they were astonished to discover that all the decorations had been pulled down from the walls and off the tree and were piled neatly in the middle of the living room floor. The presence, the Evans felt, was trying to tell them something. The colonel added another line to the emerging profile of the Tod House ghost. "The ghost," he wrote, "also hated Christmas." [1]

While the Evans never saw the ghost themselves, there was one especially terrifying incident the year after they had taken possession of Tod House. As was their habit during the Second World War, Colonel and Mrs. Evans invited two airmen into their home to spend weekend leave.

Since neither man seemed to be the squeamish type, Mrs. Evans elected to put them in the one bedroom that received little use — the one that the couple had used briefly as a master bedroom a year earlier. The room had been completely refurbished with new wallpaper and even a fresh paint trim. It must have seemed absurd not to use it for guests.

When Mrs. Evans arose the next day, she was surprised to find the guest room empty. It appeared to have been vacated suddenly: the blankets and sheets lay in a twisted mess on the bed. It was only long after the morning sun had risen that the Evans's guests returned. According to them, the night had begun normally enough, but before it ended both were frightened almost out of their wits. The account of one of the servicemen was later recorded in a Victoria newspaper:

> We had been asleep for several hours when I suddenly awoke. I can't really describe what woke me, although it sounded like the rattling of chains. Over in the corner stood an Indian woman, her hands held out toward me in such a manner that she seemed to be pleading with me to help her.
>
> On her arms and legs were what looked like fetters. She kept looking at me, her hands outstretched and saying something that I couldn't catch. As suddenly as she appeared she was gone. I'll never forget the sight.[2]

The story of the chained Indian woman was particularly interesting to the colonel. During his research into the history of Tod House he had learned that it was rumoured that one of Tod's Indian wives had gone mad and was kept chained in an upstairs bedroom. The story related by the Evans's unfortunate guest (the second man apparently woke up only after the figure had disappeared) lent validity to this tale, since the man had no notion of the history of Tod House.

While the ghost had caused them considerable anguish when they first moved into the old house, the couple gradually became accustomed to its presence. If not exactly part of the family, it seemed like an (usually) unobtrusive lodger padding silently about the house. At times having the ghost about was even pleasant. "There's one thing about it," Mrs. Evans observed. "You're never lonely with these invisible personages around. I don't ever feel I am alone."[3]

However, for those unaccustomed to the ghost, an encounter with it could be frightening. The Evans had lived in the house several years when they decided to hold a New Year's Eve party. The evening was well under way when suddenly a guest noticed something strange. In the kitchen was a massive stone fireplace, part of the original house. Set in the stonework was a hook upon which Mrs. Evans had suspended a porcelain biscuit jar. As the guests watched almost mesmerized, the jar swung to and fro on the hook. The movement continued unabated for about 35 minutes before finally stopping. Despite Colonel Evans's attempt to reassure everyone that it was really quite a routine event at Tod House, the moving biscuit jar severely upset a number of guests that night.

The result was that the Tod House ghost, which had been the subject of neighbourhood gossip for many years, suddenly became a matter of broader public interest. Victoria and Vancouver newspapers picked up the story, while reporters trekked out to Oak Bay to interview the Evans. Some journalists were even fortunate enough to witness strange events themselves, including the mysterious moving cookie jar and the cellar door that opened by itself. Other reporters succeeded in tracking down the previous owner of the house, Mrs. E. C. Turner. Mrs. Turner who, with her daughter, had occupied Tod House from 1929 until she sold it in 1944, was no less familiar with the ghost than Colonel and Mrs. Evans.

"Sometimes I would awake at night feeling a presence in my room," reported Mrs. Turner. "The door would slowly open although I couldn't see anything. I am still fully convinced that

there was someone there." If Mrs. Turner couldn't see anything, there was one member of her household that apparently
could — her cat. And what that little animal saw must have
been scary, indeed. "At night the cat would suddenly growl and
arch her back and her fur would stand up," Mrs. Turner recalled. "I feel sure that she saw something that I could not
see."[4]

What was interesting, also, was that Mrs. Turner shared
Colonel and Mrs. Evans's feelings regarding the "eerie room."
Like the Evans, neither the woman nor her daughter would
spend the night in that room. However, unlike the Evans who
grew accustomed to the ghost, Mrs. Turner found that it wore
her down. "Sometimes as I walked along the passage way, I felt
that someone was walking behind me. It got very tiresome," she
confessed.

Suddenly the Evans were offered all sorts of explanations and
advice from psychic experts. Wrote one medium: "It is an indication that in the past someone was terribly unhappy in the
house and has returned now to try and find the happiness they
missed."[5]

However, no one was quite sure how to exorcise the unhappy
ghost from the premises. One expert advised leaving a pad and
pencil in plain view, in order that the ghost could communicate.
Another suggested leaving out a pail of water, because sometimes that placated a restless soul from the "other world." In
this case, neither approach was successful. Doors continued to
open, hats flew, and jars, alas, rocked.

Canada's fascination with the Tod House ghost reached its
peak early in 1947, when the story was aired on the CBC. By
then the owners were subjected to a continual stream of cars
driving slowly by to get a look at the haunted house. The Evans,
too, would be startled to see little children with their faces
pushed up against the glass of the downstairs windows, looking
for the ghost. After the broadcast, the Evans were inundated
with mail. While many of the letters were from cranks, a number of people wrote to express their sympathy. One measure of
the popularity of the ghost house was a letter the colonel re-

ceived from Oakville, Ontario. The address read simply, "Colonel Evans, the Haunted House, Victoria." It found its way to the Evans's house without difficulty.

For a retired couple like the Evans, the publicity associated with the haunted house was most unwelcome, and they were relieved when public interest began to fade. In early 1947, the colonel undertook much-needed renovations to the dwelling. Among the planned improvements was the installation of an oil-burning furnace to replace the old wood and coal burner.

Colonel Evans hired two men to do the difficult labour, digging a very deep hole beside the front porch to accommodate the oil-storage tank. When they had reached a depth of seven feet, the shovel of one of the men struck something unexpected. It was a soft, porous material that easily crumbled in the hand. The colonel studied it closely. Despite its terribly deteriorated condition, there was no mistaking what it was — pieces of a human skeleton.

The colonel asked the workmen to uncover all the bones, but the men refused. Even after he offered them a substantial bonus to finish the job, the men continued to demand more. They were, of course, aware that Tod House already had a frightening reputation and, in the end, the colonel had to do the job himself.

What he found in the ground by his house was a human skeleton, complete except, curiously, for the head. Colonel Evans had the bones examined by an anatomist. The remains, it was reported, were those of an Oriental or native Indian woman. Because of their poor condition, it was difficult to estimate how long the bones had been buried, but certainly more than 50 years. Similarly, the cause of death could not be determined. As to why the bones were so badly decomposed, it was the opinion of the anatomist that the woman's body had been buried in quick-lime.

Some people maintained that the bones were evidence that old John Tod had been involved in smuggling Orientals into the area, but there was not a shred of evidence to support this thesis. It seemed more likely that the unfortunate woman was

someone close to John Tod: someone, if the rumours were correct, who had known long years of torment and madness.
There is one more intriguing twist to this story. Once the bones were removed from the unmarked grave, the haunting of Tod House abruptly ceased. Although a number of mediums continued to predict the return of the spirit to John Tod's old farmhouse, it never came back to haunt Colonel and Mrs. Evans. Yet the loss of their visitor must have been a mixed blessing. As the Evans admitted, they had grown used to the presence of their ghost.

* * * * *

There is a brief footnote to the Tod House haunting. In 1971, after the colonel's death, the property changed hands again. For the new owner, however, the value of Tod House as a historical site had to be weighed against the cost of maintaining such an old building. Also, at a time of rapidly escalating real estate prices, the large piece of property on which the house stood was valuable indeed.

On June 24, 1974, the house was again in the news when the Oak Bay Municipal Council moved to declare Tod House a heritage landmark, which meant that no major changes could be made to the structure without the approval of council. Some time later the house was purchased by the municipality of Oak Bay and the provincial government. Currently, it is administered by a board appointed jointly by the two levels of government.

Has the ghost returned to Tod House as many seers have predicted? No, according to the present tenant-caretaker, Chester Rufh. Since they moved into the house no one in the Rufh household has seen, heard, or felt anything unusual.

Stately Old Haunts

As some of British Columbia's stately old houses are bought up by the government for use as museums, art galleries and the like, the "presences" of private homes become the "ghosts" of public institutions. Many of those involved in the operation of museums or galleries are not keen on mentioning their resident ghosts, but the ghosts are there, nonetheless.

Irving House

One historic old British Columbia residence claiming a ghost or two is New Westminster's Irving House. Begun in 1862 by the Royal Engineers, the 14-room home stands on the side of a hill overlooking the Fraser River. The first owner of the house was William Irving, a Scots riverboat captain who immigrated to British Columbia via Oregon in 1859. Captain Irving established his family in Victoria, initially, and began a ferry service between the Fraser River goldfields and the coast. The Irving family occupied their new house on the mainland in 1864. Captain Irving, however, did not have many years to enjoy his home; eight years later, at the age of 56, he succumbed to pneumonia.

The house remained in the possession of Captain Irving's descendants until 1950, when it was sold to the city of New Westminster as a historic site. Today Irving House has been

Irving House. (COURTESY OF NEW WESTMINSTER PUBLIC LIBRARY)

painstakingly restored to represent the period between 1864 and 1890. Fortunately, in 1950, city fathers had the good sense to purchase the furnishings, and many of the items in the house are Irving originals. Irving House is now part of New Westminster's museum complex on Royal Avenue.

The museum's curator, Archie Miller, has had a few strange experiences in the old house. He has occupied an apartment in the dwelling since 1973, and over the years has become familiar with every creak and groan the old house makes but, as he states, there are some occurrences that cannot be readily explained.

Early one morning in 1980, Mr. Miller was awakened by the low growling of his Norwegian elkhound, Sapper, who was beside his bed. The dog was very agitated. Mr. Miller could see his fur bristling. "I knew something wasn't right."[1]

At first the curator assumed that there was an intruder on the property — someone walking on the porch — but as he listened, he realized the sound wasn't outside the house; it was inside. Above his head he could hear footsteps in the upstairs hall. The noise was quite distinctive, Mr. Miller recalled — like the sound of a full-grown man pacing the hall. Mr. Miller and his dog proceeded up the staircase. He ordered Sapper to guard the bottom of the stairs while he checked the outside of the house. He could find no evidence of a break-in. He returned to the bottom of the stairs, but by then the footsteps had stopped. He went upstairs and again there was no sign of a break-in.

As Mr. Miller thought about the incident later, he continued to be puzzled. "It made no sense that someone would be walking back and forth above me. After all, it would have been strange behaviour for a thief, pacing like that." Moreover, even if the intruder had succeeded in sneaking in earlier, there was no way he could manage to escape from the locked house.

"I've had people tell me it's only the house creaking, but I've lived here over 15 years and I've come to know the sounds that belong and the sounds that don't belong. And these sounds definitely didn't belong."

There was another incident about a year later. Mr. Miller and two tour guides were just closing up after the last visitor had left, when suddenly one of the women called out that she heard something upstairs. Mr. Miller's first thought, of course, was that one of the visitors had stayed back and hidden somewhere. As the guides waited below, Mr. Miller went up the main staircase.

Suddenly he was aware that something was happening. "As I approached the top two or three stairs, I had the feeling someone was coming down." Instinctively he flattened himself against the wall to let whomever it was pass by. Quite shaken, he called down to the guides at the bottom of the steps, asking if they saw anything. "No," they said, peering up at the curator who was still pressed against the wall. "But what are you doing?" As in the previous incident, Mr. Miller's search of the house revealed no intruder or sign of a break-in.

Mr. Miller, himself, has not seen anything unusual in Irving House, but some visitors have, on a number of occasions. Some time ago, there were two different reports of similar ghostly sightings — a small woman wearing an old-fashioned, dark-coloured dress — in the house. Interestingly, at the time of the incidents, both witnesses reported hearing the rustle of clothes. The museum staff found these occurrences interesting because they came from two people unfamiliar with the history of the Irving House ghost, yet their descriptions of the spectre were almost identical.

There have been other reports. Some time ago, before Mr. Miller became curator, a little girl, about four years old, rushed up to her mother while they were touring the restored house and, pointing to one of the cordoned-off bedrooms, said "If I'm not allowed to go in there, why is that man allowed to lie on the bed?" The child's mother saw no one, but she noted that the bed had been mussed up in a manner that suggested a full-grown person had been lying on it. As staff members noted, there was certainly no adult in the house who was likely to lie on one of the carefully arranged exhibits.

Unlike presences in other houses, the Irving House ghosts are the gentle kind. Indeed, the Irvings were a close family, and the house, over the years, knew more joy than sorrow. Who are the ghosts of Irving House? Many believe that the female spectre is either Elizabeth Irving, Captain Irving's wife, or their daughter, Mary. Both women spent many years in the house and were very attached to it. Mrs. Irving continued to live in the house for 13 years after the death of the captain; however, in 1885 she moved to Portland, Oregon, where she remarried. It was said this second marriage ended badly, and it is possible she longed for the happier days in her New Westminster home. She died in Portland in 1922.

The Irvings' eldest daughter, Mary, married Thomas Briggs in 1874. Prior to Mrs. Irving's move to Portland, Thomas Briggs purchased the Irving family home from his mother-in-law and the Briggs raised nine children there. Mary Briggs remained in the house until her death in 1931.

There is still the question of the heavy footsteps upstairs. Some believe they are the footsteps of a man crushed by a wagonload of wood on the street near the house in 1871. The badly injured man was carried into Irving House where he died a short time later. A more likely candidate for the footsteps, however, is Captain Irving himself. The captain was a man of tremendous drive, who would not have left this earth willingly, and there is more evidence: apparently he had the habit of pacing. On his ships, others noted that he frequently paced the entire length of the quarterdeck. It is possible that it was the captain's ghost that Mr. Miller and his dog, Sapper, heard so distinctly that night.

There was, incidentally, one occasion involving a rather un-

Captain William Irving. (COURTESY OF NEW WESTMINSTER PUBLIC LIBRARY)

pleasant spectre when Mr. Miller was away from the house on a trip. A friend of his, a big burly fellow who was not afraid of anything, offered to house-sit while the curator was gone. All went well until one evening the man believed he heard a creaking noise in the house. Unsure of what was going on, he began to search. When he came into the front hall, he met something entirely unexpected: the figure of a man standing on the front porch, looking through the glass of the door. The man was plainly visible and as Mr. Miller's friend later reported, he did not look happy at all. The house-sitter was so shaken by the figure he ran to St. Mary's Hospital next door to Irving House, and it was some time before he regained his composure and returned to the old dwelling.

Some would argue that there was nothing supernatural about the incident at all, that Mr. Miller's friend had simply seen a prowler looking in the front-door window. However, according to Mr. Miller, there's one problem with that explanation. The glass in the door is opaque, and it is normally quite impossible to tell who is standing on the front porch.

Point Ellice House

"I stood in the drawing room of the old house, home to three generations of the O'Reilly family, trying to come to a decision. I had an uncanny feeling I was not alone." [2]

The year was 1965, and the decision facing Inez O'Reilly and her husband, John, was crucial to the continued existence of Point Ellice House. As heir to the century-old dwelling which had originally been built by his grandfather, Peter O'Reilly, John had received a generous offer for the property. If he and his wife accepted the offer, it would mean Point Ellice House would fall to the wrecker's ball. While the couple would feel the loss of the house as a severe blow, maintaining a dwelling so old was also a great responsibility. If they decided to keep Point Ellice House, the dilapidated old structure would have to undergo considerable restoration.

Point Ellice House. (COURTESY OF BC ARCHIVES)

In the end, however, the couple made what they felt was the only right decision — somehow they would find the money for repairs. Point Ellice House would be saved for a little while longer. It would be a tragedy to lose this wonderful piece of Victoria history, and also, Mrs. O'Reilly felt that she and John were not the only residents of Point Ellice House. The ghosts who occupied the one-storey, 15-room structure were not disposed to losing their home either.

Point Ellice House, with Irving House, shares the distinction of being one of the oldest houses in the province. Built between 1865 and 1867, the dwelling was in its day one of the finest homes in Victoria. O'Reilly, a native of County Meath, Ireland, came to British Columbia in 1859. Because of his experience in the Irish Revenue Police, young O'Reilly was made the stipendiary magistrate for the community of Fort Langley and within two years, Governor James Douglas had appointed him magistrate and gold commissioner for the all-important Cariboo district.

While O'Reilly spent much of his time in the interior of British Columbia, he chose to have his house built in the civilized city of Victoria. Peter and his wife Caroline — he had married the sister of British Columbia's first lieutenant-governor, Sir Joseph Trutch — built their home on the banks of the narrow inlet known as the Gorge. There the O'Reillys raised their family, two boys and a girl. In the 1880s and 90s the house was the scene of elaborate parties and other social events attended by the cream of Victoria society.

Kathleen O'Reilly, daughter of Peter and Caroline, never married, remaining at Point Ellice House until her death in 1945. It is not surprising, then, that there are those who feel Miss O'Reilly remains even now within its walls.

As the years passed the O'Reilly family faced a considerable problem: the house was in the wrong place. While the location had once been singularly attractive, overlooking as it did the Selkirk Water of Victoria's Inner Harbour, the other fine residences which had shared the locale were sold and pulled down to make way for industry. By the mid 1960s, Point Ellice House was among the last of the grand old homes that had been built there.

In 1967, after spending two years rebuilding the house, John and Inez O'Reilly opened Point Ellice House as a private museum. As at Irving House, some visitors saw more than the curators intended. Soon after the house was opened to the public, Mrs. O'Reilly received a complaint from one woman visitor regarding the ghosts which had frightened her small granddaughter. "You should warn people that the house is haunted," the angry woman demanded. "We should sue you. It's very dangerous."[3]

There were other instances, however, where the ghosts were helpful; in one case, a mysterious woman in an old-fashioned blue dress showed a visiting family around the house. There was no one in the house at the time that fit the family's description, but the dress was real enough — their description matched one that was once worn by Kathleen O'Reilly. Another time, two male visitors claimed that they had seen the apparition of a woman who fit Kathleen's description waiting for them as they arrived. When the young men left, they said the figure followed them down the road.

The ghost of Miss O'Reilly does not seem to be alone. In 1971, a well-known American psychic, Suzie Smith, paid a visit, and she could sense not one presence, but as many as four. They were there, it seems, to help keep the museum tidy, although Ms. Smith didn't explain how the ghosts accomplished this. One of the presences haunting the house is likely to be Caroline O'Reilly, the first mistress of Point Ellice House. The elder Mrs. O'Reilly was very attached to her home, so it would not be surprising that she has remained behind. However, who the other two presences are is not clear.

In 1974, the house was sold to the provincial government and is now administered by the Ministry of Municipal Affairs, Recreation and Culture. Since then, there have been no ghostly goings-on reported by museum staff members.

Fairacres: The Burnaby Art Gallery

"If the walls of Fairacres could talk, they would weep," Vancouver *Sun* reporter John Armstrong concluded in 1987.[4] Indeed, the history of the huge, three-storey mansion overlooking the lake is one of pain and sadness. There were a few good years of course, but the 80-year-old structure seems to have retained within its walls considerably more sorrow than happiness. The ghosts who haunt this building, which is now the Burnaby Art Gallery, are lugubrious creatures, aptly fitting the old home's sad past.

When Fairacres was completed in 1909, Vancouver was enjoying an economic boom. Writers boldly predicted that an industrial Vancouver would become the "Pittsburgh of the Pacific," while businessmen saw no end to the city's rapid growth. A wealthy and powerful business class was emerging; one member of this group was a Vancouver insurance and real estate tycoon, Henry Ceperley. Ceperley was born in New York state in 1851 and moved to British Columbia in 1886. In 1909, Ceperley retired, and with his second wife, Grace, decided to build a country mansion in what was then rural Burnaby. Although not many miles from Vancouver, the huge Tudor-style mansion seemed remote. The dwelling overlooked a small lake which included waterfowl and fish. "He is a most genial and companionable gentleman," wrote a biographer in 1914, "and has gained a host of warm friends during his residence in the northwest."[5] Indeed, Ceperley seemed to enjoy the role of country squire, entertaining Vancouver society with extravagant parties at the mansion. It seems likely that he spent a large part of his considerable fortune through this expansive lifestyle. Mrs. Ceperley seemed to prefer a quieter life. She was a very warm, caring person who spent many hours tending her beautiful garden (which was actually maintained by her Chinese gardener) and feeding the wild birds which flocked to the area.

The Ceperleys lived at Fairacres for only ten years. In 1919, Mrs. Ceperley died suddenly and when her will was probated it was discovered that she owned the house. Under the terms of her will, the mansion would remain at the disposal of her husband, but when he died, the money realized by the sale of the house should be used to provide a children's playground at Stanley Park. Ceperley, faced with maintaining the huge house only for himself, first leased it, and then sold it outright in 1922, ignoring the provisions of his wife's will. The Stanley Park playground was not built.

The new owner of Fairacres was Henry Buscombe who held the property only a few years before it was sold to a family named Bogardus. The huge house must have been enormously expensive to maintain as a private residence, even for Vancouver's wealthiest citizens, and eventually it was turned into an annex for the Vancouver General Hospital's tuberculosis ward. In the years before the introduction of anti-tubercular drugs, the mansion *cum* hospital was a place of considerable suffering and misery. After the annex was closed, Fairacres was briefly reconverted into a private residence and became home to Mr.

and Mrs. Alexander Munro. In 1939 the house was sold again. The new owner of the estate was a Benedictine religious order from Mount Angel Seminary in Oregon. (The total price, incidentally, for the mansion and property was only $13,000.) Despite the order's strict discipline, and the fact that the now middle-aged dwelling was inadequately heated, many of those who were at Westminster Priory (as it was called) during the 1940s and early 1950s have fond memories of their time there. In 1954, however, the order moved to a new abbey a few miles from Mission, and the Burnaby property was resold.

The next owner was an unorthodox religious cult calling itself the Temple of the More Abundant Life. In 1959, the Vancouver *Sun* exposed the leader of the sect, "Archbishop John I," as a convicted bigamist named William Franklin Wolsey who had a string of extortion and wife-beating charges throughout the eastern United States. Archbishop John, the newspaper revealed, had been consecrated in London in the year 1955 by Archbishop Percival Nicholson, Primate of the Ancient Catholic Church (and former waiter at London's Savoy Hotel). Moreover, the impressive degrees which Wolsey so proudly displayed were shown to be entirely bogus — purchased from British and American degree mills.

There were also disturbing rumours about the practices in the live-in church school. The archbishop's ideas on education could be described as bizarre. The male teachers were required to wear beards because facial hair acts as an "antenna", allowing the educator to pick up the vibrations emitted by the universe. However, there was a darker side to the school. The archbishop had a vicious temper which was frequently unleashed on the children at the school. On one occasion when a six-year-old boy with a slight speech impediment couldn't keep up with the other children during the recital of the Lord's Prayer, Wolsey was enraged, and the boy was so traumatized by the incident that he reverted to baby talk.

In the face of a government probe into his educational methods, the archbishop closed his school in 1960. Four years later his church collapsed and Wolsey fled to the United States.

While the whole truth of what happened at the school will never be known, those who have investigated the Fairacres hauntings conclude that many occurrences concern children. After the collapse of the "Temple," Fairacres took on a new role: that of a university dormitory. In an era when "doing your own thing" meant rejecting tradition and everything the past stood for, the once-beautiful interior of the structure was subjected to considerable defacement by the students. In 1966 the building was purchased by the municipality of Burnaby, but attempts by the local council to oust the students met with resistance. Shouting Marxist slogans they erected barricades, waved banners, and even set fire to the beautiful hardwood floor in the billiard room. While the students eventually lost the battle, the greatest casualty was the once-magnificent mansion.

In 1967, Fairacres was reopened as Burnaby's project in honour of the Canadian Centennial: a new art gallery to serve the citizens of the municipality. At last the old mansion had regained some of the dignity it had lost in recent years, but the damage was not all physical. Fairacres was now haunted by the pain and suffering of its past; the gallery, it seems, has its complement of ghosts.

Actually, the first report of strange occurrences came about the time the gallery first opened, when a night watchman reported seeing the spectre of Grace Ceperley upstairs. She was wearing an old-fashioned, long, flowing white dress, but even in the dim light he could tell it was transparent. The third floor, it should be noted, was originally designated as the children's rooms and Mrs. Ceperley was very fond of children.

There were also rumours during the early years of the gallery that other staff members have seen what many feel is the ghost of Mrs. Ceperley. The wispy outline of a woman in either a grey or a blue evening dress has been reported walking along the open gallery area. One female staff member, it was said, even tried to talk to the apparition, but later refused to discuss the incident. As might be expected, many of the art gallery's employees have been reluctant to talk about such episodes. To their credit some staff have freely described their experiences in the building. Maria Guerrero had been working in an office on the second floor for some time before she learned that the third floor was unused. Above her head, she frequently heard footsteps walking across the creaking wooden floors and up staircases, and the scraping noise made by furniture as it was moved along the floor. "I didn't worry because I thought someone lived up there," she said. "The noises were so real."[6]

Early one evening in 1984 the programs officer, Carol Defina, waited alone at the gallery's reception desk for other staff to arrive for a meeting. Suddenly behind her she heard a rustling sound, as if someone was swishing a taffeta or satin dress or maybe even a crinoline. The sound was quite distinctive. As she later recalled:

> I was intent on preparing my notes and I heard a noise. I wasn't frightened, I looked over [to where the noise was coming from] and there was nothing there. About four minutes later the sound grew louder. My intuition warned me that something was trying to communicate. I knew that there was something there that was not of this world.[7]

Ms. Defina took her keys and waited for the others in her car. From then on she refused to work alone at the gallery during the evening.

Many staff believe that the old building is haunted by a second ghost, a man seen standing at the top of the staircase. There have been other strange occurrences as well. Mark Stevens was working on the main floor one evening in 1984, preparing the walls for an exhibition. One other staff member, Robert Lagasse, was working in the basement. Because it was after closing, the building's alarm system was turned on. As he worked, Mr. Stevens became aware of the noise of someone walking diagonally from a bedroom balcony across to the opposite end on the second floor. Because there was no carpeting on the floor at the time, the sound was quite distinctive: someone in stocking feet or maybe soft slippers was pressing down on the creaking old floor.

Burnaby Art Gallery. (PHOTOGRAPH BY D.M. BELYK)

Mr. Stevens phoned his colleague, Mr. Lagasse, in the basement. Together the two men searched the building thoroughly, but to their surprise, no one was hiding there. As far as Mr. Stevens was concerned it was impossible. "If [the intruder] went out the french doors the alarm would have gone off. There were no open windows, and even if there were, it's a long two-storey drop, 25 feet or more."[8]

A year earlier, Mr. Lagasse had had his own unnerving experience while working late in the basement removing prints from their frames. The job required the use of a hammer and a screwdriver. When he had separated a large number of prints and frames he moved the art work to the floor, out of his way. When he turned around again he found his hammer and screwdriver weren't on the bench where he left them, but were hanging up in their proper place on the tool rack. To Mr. Lagasse the incident did not seem particularly unusual. He thought that he may have absent-mindedly replaced the tools in the rack. He picked out his hammer and screwdriver and continued to work on the prints and frames.

After a few minutes he picked up the separated frames and took them to the storage room to be put away. When he arrived there he reached in his pocket for his keys. As he did so he noticed that the padlock on the door was swinging to and fro on its own. The lock continued its motion for as long as Mr. Lagasse watched, which was several minutes. When he returned to his workbench his tools were again not where he had left them. They had been returned to their place in the rack. "Then I got this cold feeling on the back of my neck... I knew something was different, the atmosphere had changed."[9]

By late 1985, the Vancouver press was beginning to take an interest in the "ghosts" at the Burnaby Art Gallery. In December of that year, Vancouver *Daily Province* assistant city editor, Damian Inwood, and a photographer, Les Brazso, arranged to spend the night in the reputedly haunted gallery. After an unremarkable evening, the two made themselves as comfortable as possible in the billiard room. Before climbing into their sleeping bags, they set up a small voice-activated tape recorder, just in case.

Some time in the night the reporter awoke abruptly. "I felt that something had nudged my subconscious, trying to attract my attention, and I was suddenly afraid," he wrote later. "A chilling presence seemed to be pushing its way into the room and filling it."[10]

The newspaper man tried to scream, but nothing happened; he tried to move but found he couldn't bring his body to a sitting position. He looked across at his companion but he was fast asleep in his sleeping bag. Then suddenly the terrible weight of the presence seemed to lift. The icy chill left the air and everything was back to normal.

Mr. Inwood remained awake the remainder of the night. In the morning he checked his voice-activated recorder. As he wrote later: "I expected to hear myself crying out in my sleep.

Instead, sandwiched between our conversations, was a weird warble followed by hissing silence." Whether it was an ordinary nightmare or something more, the incident was very unsettling. The reporter made no plans to spend another night there.

Two years later a Vancouver *Sun* reporter, John Armstrong, repeated the experiment. For Mr. Armstrong, however, the night was uneventful.

An obvious question concerns the identity of the ghosts who haunt the gallery and one candidate is Grace Ceperley. That the provisions of her will were not carried out regarding the bequest of money for the children's playground at Stanley Park may be the reason for this restless spirit. Ghosts elsewhere have needed even less excuse to do their haunting. There are apparently many other ghosts who haunt Fairacres, though, strangely, as far as is known, there were no tragic deaths there of the kind that seem to leave a psychic "impression" on a structure for years after the event.

There may be one clue to the other presences there. Early in 1987, a well-known psychic, Joan Fontaine, visited Fairacres with a television crew. Ms. Fontaine's "reading" of the gallery was later broadcast on the CBC, and as might be expected, the psychic pronounced the gallery a very troubled place. She could sense children pleading for help, but she said more, not all of which was broadcast on the program. As part of his final report, the departing gallery director, Roger Boulet, wrote that Ms. Fontaine had expressed the impression that much of the unhappiness associated with the house concerned the abuse of children. "These episodes," he concluded, "seem to relate to the occupancy of the building by the Society of the Foundation for a More Abundant Life." [11]

The current gallery director, Lina Jabra, states that she has experienced no strange incidents since taking the position on June 1, 1988. Perhaps the wonderful light which arises from the beautiful art work hanging on exhibit in the gallery has overcome the darkness of Fairacres' past.

* * * * *

36

Incidentally, Fairacres is not the first haunted art gallery in British Columbia. During the 1950s, Victoria's Norfolk Gallery on Broad Street was operated by Theo Hare. Hare was a popular figure in Victoria art circles and his sudden death one day when he was working in his gallery was a shock to all those who knew him. In due course the gallery was reopened under a new name by Katie Bloomfield. Soon afterwards, Mrs. Bloomfield discovered that the former owner had not exactly vacated the premises. As she recalled:

> I saw him one night.... I had to go down the corridor past [Mr. Hare's old office] and he appeared in the doorway. I couldn't go into the kitchen some nights because I felt someone was there. The hair stood up on my neck.[12]

According to Mrs. Bloomfield the spectre wasn't solid but was the "shape of a man" leaning on the frame of the door. She added ominously that she felt there was "something else" upstairs, and she wouldn't go there at night, or even in the daytime for that matter if she was alone.

A few years later, the gallery was taken over and operated by Chris Phillips and his wife, Alma. Like Mrs. Bloomfield, they soon discovered that there were strange goings-on at the gallery. Both Mr. and Mrs. Phillips claimed to have seen the misty figure of a man in the corridor by Mr. Hare's old office. The couple was not the only witnesses: one day their four-year-old son reported that a strange man had come into his room at night and sat on his bed. The living quarters the Phillips family occupied were secure, and there was no way that the boy's visitor could have been a living human being. While his parents were much disturbed by the occurrence, the little boy thought nothing of it.

The Phillips family closed the gallery in 1960 and moved away from Victoria. As far as is known, there were no further reports of the spectral presence at the Broad Street address.

The Williams Street Haunting: Portrait of a Ghost

Haunted portraits are a universal theme of many ghost stories. For some reason, ghosts appear to have a particular affinity for such works of art. Yet the story of one unusual British Columbia picture is even stranger than other portrait tales. The picture in question here is not entirely the work of a living person — it is said that the finishing touches were supplied by a ghost.

In the mid 1960s, the huge three-storey structure on Chilliwack's Williams Street could have easily been mistaken for the set of a Gothic horror movie, but the old house wasn't a Hollywood prop; it was entirely real, and in the winter of 1965 it became home to Douglas and Hetty Fredrickson and their family.

The big house was just right for a large family — the Fredricksons had five children — but there was another advantage as well. The old house had character of the kind that would inspire an artist like Mrs. Fredrickson. It was the perfect place for the new owner to set up her studio. However, as the Fredricksons were about to discover, the house's "character" went beyond providing the artist with inspiration.

Mrs. Fredrickson had not been in the house long when it became apparent to her that something was wrong. The couple intended to use one of the large upstairs bedrooms which overlooked Williams Street for guests, but it was not possible. It was this room that seemed to be the centre of the haunting.

At night footsteps would be heard on the stairs leading to the upper floor. The new owners would, of course, check through the house, but there was never anyone there. When Mrs. Fredrickson examined the guest bedroom the following morning, dresser drawers which she made sure were closed the previous night would be open, while the heavy old iron bedstead would be moved about the room. The bed actually seemed to be restless, moving night after night until it finally found the right location under a window.

There were other incidents that were frightening, like the sound of breathing in an apparently empty room and, strangely, the smell of perfume. The Fredricksons would suddenly be aware that perfume was permeating the room.

In the beginning, at least, Mrs. Fredrickson was more puzzled than frightened. "I am not afraid," she remarked, "but I

The Fredrickson house. (COURTESY OF HETTY FREDRICKSON)

would like to find a logical explanation."[1] The problem was that as far as she could determine, there simply wasn't any rational interpretation. Moreover, something else was happening which Mrs. Fredrickson found extremely distressing. Soon after moving into the house, she began having a terrible recurring nightmare. Night after night she had the same dream: the body of a woman lying on the floor of the hall upstairs. "She is sort of mummified and she has a red dress on with yellow flowers, a cheap cotton dress, and she is terrified," explained Mrs. Fredrickson.[2]

Mrs. Fredrickson found the haunting combined with her recurring dream very upsetting. However, she was not without considerable personal fortitude, and after putting up with the disturbances for five months, Mrs. Fredrickson was determined to get to the bottom of the mystery. She undertook a two-step plan against the ghost. First, she would dig into the history of the house to discover if any tragic event had occurred there, particularly something involving a woman. "I intend to find out if someone has been living here with this dress on," she told reporters, "because I can describe it absolutely."

Second, she prepared to meet the ghost on its own turf. Beginning the last week in May 1966, Mrs. Fredrickson decided to wait up for the ghost. Taking her sketch pad, a pencil and a candle to the "haunted" spare bedroom, she planned to sit all night until the ghost appeared. Then she would draw its picture. Why draw its picture? As an artist, Mrs. Fredrickson became convinced that simply rendering its likeness on paper or canvas would rid the house of the spectre.

For two nights nothing untoward happened. On the third night Mrs. Fredrickson became aware of something. Near the window she saw what she described as "a sort of light," but the misty luminescence took on no clear definition. "It looked like a cloudy figure," she later recalled. "It was the shape of a human being, but no details, no face." As she stared at the glowing shape before her, Mrs. Fredrickson wondered if it was no more than a product of her imagination. "I closed my eyes and opened them and it was still there. I didn't dare get up. When it went, it just disappeared." The ghost was more than a visual experience. Soon after it had gone, she was aware of something pleasant in the air, "I could definitely smell perfume."

Although for her purposes, Mrs. Fredrickson's experience with the ghost was unsatisfactory — she was not able to see the features of the apparition clearly — she was determined to render the image on canvas. She decided to combine the faceless form of the ghost with the image of the dead girl in the floral print dress, from her dream, but she had trouble "capturing" the elusive ghost on canvas. In the end, to signify her difficulty with the project, Mrs. Fredrickson left half the head uncompleted, putting in the eye on only one side of the face. The artist spent a number of days working on the portrait and when it was done, she had produced a very large canvas — it measured about four feet by six feet — of the "ghost".

About a week after painting the picture, Mrs. Fredrickson became aware that, like the portrait in Oscar Wilde's famous novel, *The Picture of Dorian Gray*, it was beginning to change on its own. However, unlike the work in the Wilde allegory, the picture was recasting not the age of the subject, but its sex. "The woman's portrait is changing to that of a man," she told the reporters who were now beginning to take a considerable interest in the story. "I haven't touched the painting but it is gradually changing." [3]

It was, Mrs. Fredrickson maintained, definitely not the face she had painted earlier. The details on the uncompleted side of the face were beginning to fill in on their own and the changes were quite dramatic. The dark side of the face lightened considerably, and took on an eyelid and a nostril, as well as an outline of the cheek. The painted side of the face changed also. What appeared to be a very thin moustache was visible under the nose, while heavier lines of shadow hardened the face. The change in the portrait was particularly strange because Mrs. Fredrickson had painted the face of the woman she saw so vividly in her dreams. The person in the cotton print dress lying on the hall floor was obviously not a man.

About the same time as she discovered the alterations to her painting, Mrs. Fredrickson heard several rumours about the history of the house. One story she was told concerned an old man who had committed suicide in the house a number of years earlier. Apparently who he was, or why he had taken his own life, was not known at the time, but as far as Mrs. Fredrickson was concerned, it did reveal that the old house had a violent history.

Another rumour, about a woman who was supposedly murdered and bricked up in a chimney, seemed to strike a responsive chord with the artist. This could explain the woman in the print dress in her dreams. However, the Fredricksons came to the conclusion that the rumour was too fantastic to be true. Terrible things like that just didn't happen in quiet little farming

Hetty Fredrickson's portrait of the ghost.
(COURTESY OF HETTY FREDRICKSON)

communities in the Fraser Valley.

The Fredricksons began a painstaking search through the old house for the remains of an old chimney. The house, the couple soon discovered, was full of surprises. After removing a wall of panelling in the attic, they found a boarded-up door, which led to the old-fashioned turret room visible from the road. While the room was found to contain only insulation and dust, Mrs. Fredrickson felt strongly that it was the setting of her terrible dreams, the place where the body of the young woman lay on the floor. Just why this room was sealed off so completely from the rest of the house was not known.

On June 1, 1966, two reporters from the Vancouver *Sun* with a friend arranged with Mrs. Fredrickson to spend the night in the "haunted" bedroom. However, with the exception of the mysterious relocation of a roll of linoleum, and some noise in the hall, the trio observed nothing strange. The ghost watch was regarded as a failure.

Mrs. Fredrickson had hoped that publicity would bring forward someone who could solve the mystery of what was happening at the old house, but the many newspaper articles seemed to provoke only considerable public speculation regarding the presence or absence of the Williams Street ghost. During the first few weeks in June "Hetty's ghost" became a popular topic in British Columbia.

On June 3, 1966, the Vancouver *Sun* published an interview with the previous owner of the Williams Street house, Mrs. Margaret Lindhout. The lady had very definite views regarding Mrs. Fredrickson and her ghost, claiming that her son had slept in the "haunted bedroom" for four years without experiencing anything unusual. While she did confirm that an old man had committed suicide in the slough at the back of the house, as far as the ghost was concerned, Mrs. Lindhout was firm. "It is all a lot of baloney," she concluded.[4]

Mrs. Fredrickson, however, was equally convinced of what she had seen and heard in the house. The picture continued to change — Mrs. Fredrickson maintained that the moustache which had only lately appeared, was now gradually disappearing and the faint outline of a beard was beginning to emerge.

In May 1966, Mrs. Fredrickson got in touch with Professor Geoffrey Riddehough of the University of British Columbia. The professor was a member of Britain's well-respected Society for Psychical Research. She arranged to show him her picture, but if reports in the press were any indication, the professor was more concerned with understanding the nature of the phenomenon which may have been in the Chilliwack house than with bringing an end to the disturbances themselves. Professor Riddehough said only that he would make a study of the incident later, but nothing more was heard from him.

On June 2, Mrs. Fredrickson announced that she would hold a séance the following Sunday to contact the spirit in her house. She had invited a clairvoyant to attend. In addition, she invited local school children accompanied by their parents to tour the house. Mrs. Fredrickson had been apprised of some of the gruesome stories concerning the "ghost picture" that were being told among the children at Chilliwack schools, and she wanted them to see for themselves that there was nothing horrible at the house. Her plan, unfortunately, turned out to be entirely too successful.

On Sunday, June 5, an estimated 700 sightseers besieged the Fredrickson house. At its height, the line of visitors extended well into the street, and the stairs leading to the front door collapsed under the weight of those waiting to be admitted. "I didn't want all the children of Chilliwack having nightmares, so I told their school they could see for themselves that there is nothing horrific about the place," an exhausted Mrs. Fredrickson explained. "But more grown-ups turned up than children. You wouldn't believe it."[5] The crowds ended any hope of holding a séance, and the clairvoyant went home early.

That Sunday was only the beginning. For the next few weeks the house was one of the province's greatest tourist attractions. The Fredricksons could do nothing but watch the hundreds of people stream past. "Some of them," observed a bewildered Mrs. Fredrickson, "must have expected the ghost to ask if they wanted tea or coffee or something."[6] By now the story of the ghost picture had been circulated beyond the boundaries of the province. A constant stream of cars, many with American licence plates, drove past the house. Mrs. Fredrickson posted "no trespassing" signs and made a public appeal that the family's right to privacy should be respected. However, the cars continued to come, and it was estimated that 200 cars a day were driving by the "ghost house."

The almost constant distraction of the crowds of visitors did not, however, dampen the activities of the ghost. "It even shows up afternoons now and will spend several hours opening and closing bureau drawers in an unused bedroom," Mrs. Fredrickson wearily observed.[7] By the end of June, only about a month after the first account of the Chilliwack ghost had reached the province's major newspapers, Mrs. Fredrickson had had enough. Being at the centre of the ghost story was hard on the entire family.

"I never wanted to turn my house into a tourist attraction," a very frustrated Mrs. Fredrickson told a reporter for the Vancouver *Daily Province*. "You would think that after a while interest would die down.'[8] Not long after that interview the Fredricksons admitted defeat. Mrs. Fredrickson had hoped to determine what was happening at the house. She had failed, but the streams of visitors were turning her life, and the lives of other members of her family, into a nightmare. The Fredricksons finally closed their doors and moved to Vancouver Island; in the late 1960s, Mrs. Fredrickson lent the now-famous haunted picture to a charity project associated with the Vancouver radio station CKNW, where it became part of the "Haunted House" exhibit at the Pacific National Exhibition. During the time it was on display, the painting was seen by thousands of fair visitors.

While it is uncertain whether the picture really changed or not, it is clear that the mood of near hysteria generated by the occurrences in the house prevented an objective evaluation of the painting. During the time when interest in the picture was at its height, the paint on the portrait had been "tested" so much by the curious public that it was being worn off.

Hetty Fredrickson, around the time of
the haunting. (COURTESY OF HETTY FREDRICKSON)

Those who were sceptical of the haunting seemed to be sup-
ported by the fact that the Fredrickson ghost story came to an
end immediately after the family left. The house stayed vacant
for some time and the property was repeatedly vandalized — so
badly that even a tub was stolen from a bathroom. Finally in
1968, Mrs. Fredrickson arranged for a group of 12 musicians to
move into the house. In exchange for free rent the young men
took care of upkeep and small repairs. During their stay, the
musicians reported seeing no ghosts. Subsequently the house
was sold and rented out to a series of tenants.

In the spring of 1972 another family moved in: a man, his
wife and eight children. The wife (who, after the Fredrickson
fiasco, didn't want to have her name mentioned in the media)
complained about doors that would bang when no one was

around and how the thermostat would be turned up to 80 degrees. One of the most striking things about the ghost or ghosts (the family believed there were three distinct entities "living" there) was that their dog, Lucky, seemed to be so afraid during these episodes. Normally he was not frightened by anything, but when doors slammed shut, Lucky could be found shaking and cowering in a corner. Very frightening, also, was the fact that, like Mrs. Fredrickson, the children of the Williams Street house were beginning to suffer from terrible nightmares.

There were now rumours of other mysterious incidents. Earlier, some people who had briefly occupied the house obtained other accommodation and moved out. When they returned to pick up the last of their things, they said that they saw, "something like a shadow moving back and forth."[9] A delivery woman for one of the department stores pulled up in front of the house to deliver a package. A woman carrying a baby suddenly appeared on the porch. The delivery woman could tell that these two were not living beings. She eventually dropped the package on the sidewalk and ran away.

In 1973 the old house was again up for sale. Reporters from the Vancouver newspapers tried to contact the owner of the house, James Kipp, to find out why the house was being sold, but they had no success. He was not available for comment. Several years later fire broke out in the basement, and within a short time the house was destroyed.

Some time after she had moved away from Williams Street, Mrs. Fredrickson recalled that at the height of the haunting craze, she was afraid to even sweep down her porch with her broom. As she admitted sadly, it was simply not wise to be caught with a broom in her hand — it would be impossible to know what one of the many little children, who always seemed to be waiting around outside the house, might imagine and say.

More Houses

Sometimes it is relatively easy to discover the details of a haunting. In the case of Tod House, for example, Colonel and Mrs. Evans spent many years in the house, and thus were able to recall many unusual happenings there. The Evans, also, although they at first didn't believe in ghosts, were careful and credible observers and were prepared to acknowledge what they had witnessed.

Unfortunately for those interested in such phenomena, well-documented hauntings of this kind are rare. Frequently, none of the inhabitants of a haunted house stay there long. Because resident ghosts tend to bring property values down, many owners will quietly sell the dwelling and move on, rather than acknowledge the truth. At other times, although people may be willing to report strange goings-on to the press, they stipulate that their address is not to be made public. While one can sympathize with the plight of these people, concealing the location makes follow-up difficult or impossible. On some occasions, too, the details of the haunting are not reported until years after the event and by that time the witnesses, now living somewhere else, have only a limited recall of what occurred.

The following stories can be classified as minor hauntings, not because the ghost, necessarily, is any less interesting, but because the history of the occurrences is all too limited.

Oscar's Tricks

When their friends George and Sandy first suggested it, Anne Houseman and her husband, Jim, thought the idea was great. George was supervising a major construction project in northern British Columbia and the couple would be gone almost two years. In the meantime, George and Sandy would let the Housemans stay in their house rent-free. Although the house on East Second Avenue in Vancouver wasn't large, it would suit the two of them. Moreover, for Anne and Jim who hoped one day to purchase their own home, this would be a chance to save some money. "There's just one slight hitch," Sandy admitted. "We've got a ghost here." [1]

It was a late December evening in 1977 when the two couples were sitting in the front room talking. The ghost — Sandy called the presence "Oscar" — was quite harmless, and should cause no difficulty. Sandy explained that Oscar seemed to enjoy entertaining the couple's children, and in the morning she would hear them laughing at the antics of the ghost.

Anne Houseman was not particularly frightened by the prospect of a ghost in the house, while her husband simply didn't believe in the supernatural. (He was to change his mind later, however.) The fact that their friends believed the house was haunted would certainly not dissuade the Housemans from moving in.

"By the way," Sandy continued, "Oscar is around now. He keeps turning off the red Christmas lights." Anne looked at the Christmas tree which was next to her chair. One of the red lights was indeed out. She reached down and gave it several turns. The light came on. Obviously it was not defective; it had simply been loosened. Several minutes later she turned around to look at the tree. All the Christmas lights were on except one: another red bulb had somehow become loose in its socket.

Before the Housemans moved in, their friends told them that they had purchased the house from an elderly couple. The couple had not mentioned anything about a resident ghost, but that would not be surprising; ghosts are not usually regarded as positive selling features. The dwelling was obviously very old, dating from close to the turn of the century. There had probably been many owners during the years and it was impossible to tell when the phenomenon originated.

The Housemans moved into the house in January 1978, and it did not take long for Oscar to make his presence known. The couple was sound asleep in the early hours of the morning when a shrill noise suddenly erupted from the kitchen. It was the whistling tea kettle that had been standing quietly on the stove when they went to bed hours earlier. There was no way it could have suddenly boiled without someone turning up the gas under it.

"Stop it, Oscar," Jim called out humorously. To the couple's surprise, the sound abruptly stopped. When Jim and Anne went into the kitchen to investigate, they found that the stove was only operating on its pilot lights, and the tea kettle was stone cold. After that when Oscar was performing similar tricks, Jim would simply call out for him to stop, and the disturbances would cease as abruptly as they had begun.

The house was very small and space was at a premium. At one time the attic had been renovated and an extra bedroom added. It was from this room that Anne would hear the noises. They sounded as if someone was wrecking the place, things falling, furniture being dragged across the floor, but when she went to check, the room was just as it had been left — nothing out of place.

On another occasion the couple was in bed when Anne heard a racket from the bathroom. It sounded as if her large metal comb had fallen into the sink and clattered around. She asked her husband to go into the bathroom and see what had happened; to his surprise the comb had not fallen into the sink. Instead, it stood where it usually was: propped up against a towel rack.

At times, however, Oscar did move things. Late one evening Anne was catching up on her vacuuming before her husband came home. In the living room she cleaned the area around the hearth where she kept an ornamental copper kettle. She had turned off the vacuum cleaner and left the room when she heard a scraping sound, as though someone was dragging the kettle along the hearth. Sure enough, the kettle had been moved from its usual place on one end of the hearth — the spot where she had seen it only minutes before — and set at the opposite side.

One of Oscar's more common tricks was to play with a fireplace poker. There were a number of tools beside the fireplace but he seemed to favour the poker. The Housemans would watch it swing back and forth for 15 or 20 minutes without stopping. Jim checked in the area of the fireplace for drafts, but he could never find anything to account for the action of the iron.

One of the strangest incidents occurred when Jim was away at a convention and his wife was home alone. She was lying in bed when she was suddenly aware of footsteps outside her door, but the sound somehow seemed to be muffled. She lay awake listening to the noises when suddenly she was aware of movement in the room. The quilt she had thrown over herself was moving. An unseen hand was tucking her in.

Like many similar hauntings, both Housemans were aware of sudden, very localized, drops in temperature. No specific room was affected (although the incidents seemed to happen more frequently downstairs than upstairs), only certain spots. By stepping only a foot away they would suddenly feel warmer.

Oscar remained with the Housemans until they moved into their own home 18 months later. As far as is known he continues his pleasant haunt of the East Vancouver house.

The Snoring Ghost

If we accept the "recording theory" to explain the activity of most ghosts, then the record almost always involves an important moment in a person's life. Often what is recorded is the last few moments of life, before the individual meets a violent death. Thus we see a victim seconds before he puts a revolver to his head, or is stabbed, strangled or poisoned by an unkind lover. This is not surprising because these may be the most important minutes in any person's life (or death). While this seems sensible enough, what can be said about a house haunted by someone snoring? The sounds of someone's last snore hardly seem important enough to be replayed through the years, but one such case occurred about the beginning of the First World War.

Margery Wighton was 15 when her father sold the family's Okanagan fruit farm and moved to a remote area on Vancouver Island. Margery's father intended to start a chicken farm on the 12 acres of uncleared land the family had purchased, but there was a problem. Their new home was still under construction. It would be about eight weeks before they could move into their home and in the meantime they needed a place to stay.

The difficulty was overcome when a local farmer offered them a shack which stood vacant on his property. The small dwelling looked far from inviting, half-hidden as it was under a wall of tall fir trees and thick underbrush. Not far from the front door the ground suddenly fell away into a deep ravine, which increased the feeling of isolation and heaviness. Inside, the cabin didn't make the new residents feel much brighter: it was a very rudely constructed affair with a small kitchen and living room and two small bedrooms upstairs. However, it was early summer, and the house was pleasantly cool in the heat. Moreover, since Margery and her parents would have to endure this shack for only a short time, everyone agreed to make the best of it.

The first few days the family spent at the site of their new home, overseeing construction. By the time they returned home and had supper, everyone was very tired and fell asleep almost immediately. About nine o'clock on the third night, Margery retired to bed as usual, leaving her father sitting in a chair in the front room, reading a book. Before she went to sleep, however, her mother came into the room and sat on the bed discussing several matters with her daughter. Abruptly, the older woman stopped in mid-sentence. They both listened to the very

familiar and comfortable sound of someone snoring. The noise
was very loud and sounded very close to where they were sitting
on the bed. "Daddy must be tired," Margery's mother remarked.[2]

By now the noise had intrigued both women. Instead of going
to sleep Margery went downstairs with her mother. In the front
room they found Margery's father sitting reading. "I thought
you were asleep," his wife said. "We heard you snoring."

"You must both be mad," he replied indignantly. "I'm reading a good book."

When the women had again climbed the stairs, they stopped
and listened. The snoring could still be heard. Margery's
mother was convinced that her husband was playing some sort
of trick on them. Both women quietly crept downstairs, thinking
they would catch him in the act of pretending to snore. What
they found instead was the man sitting in his chair, deeply
engrossed in his book. He said, "If you two think this is awfully
amusing, I don't."

Now they were thoroughly perplexed. They explained the situation to Margery's father, and reluctantly he agreed to check
upstairs; as soon as they reached Margery's room, the snoring
could be heard again.

Now it was Margery's father's turn to be puzzled. "There's
someone here," he said. "But where?" Except for the bed and a
table, the room was empty. The family searched the upper floor
completely, but nothing could be found to account for the
strange sounds. No snoring could be heard outside the doorway
to that one bedroom. Since nothing could be found inside the
house, it seemed logical to conclude that the noise arose outside. The three family members trudged outside and listened,
but no snoring could be heard. Everything outside was in fact
dead still.

The haunted snore had now upset the entire family.
Margery's father vowed not to go to sleep until he had "laid the
ghost." Margery went to bed but tossed and turned all night. In
the morning her father was no closer to a solution to the
mystery. "I'm damned if I can stand it," he admitted. The pre-

vious night he had spent hours trying to locate the noise; he still hadn't turned up anything.

The following day he went and picked up the owner of the house, and together the two men raked the roof. However, because it was not insulated or built upon a proper foundation there was really no place in the house to conceal whatever or whoever was making the maddening snoring sound.

When evening had fallen their landlord returned to see if they were again troubled by the noise. They were. "Night after night," Mrs. Wighton noted later, "our 'snorer' enjoyed his slumbers while we had little rest." Neighbours suggested all kinds of causes: chipmunks, spiders, owls, deer, and even Indian tom-toms. There was only one thing wrong with all these "solutions," however: the only place the sound could be heard was in that one small bedroom.

Margery's family accommodated the snoring as best they could. She and her mother used the larger bedroom; her father slept downstairs. The ghost snorer was given the small bedroom to itself. Life went on for everyone, just about as usual. One day a Vancouver architect, Clem Webb, arrived for a visit. Mr. Webb was a good friend of Margery's parents and they all looked forward to his arrival. It would also give them a chance to show off their haunted bedroom. With a guest staying over, the room would be pressed into service. Everyone waited in the bedroom for the snorer to begin his nightly session, but nothing happened. For the first time in six weeks the room was not filled with the sound of snoring. Webb was credited with "laying the ghost" at last.

Not long after Webb's visit, the family moved into their new home, and the snoring incident was almost forgotten. A year later, the owner of the shack ordered a new car from a Vancouver dealer. In due course the vehicle was delivered, but the farmer, never having driven before, thought it wise for the automobile delivery person to stay around a few days and give him driving lessons. This was agreed to, but because the farmer lacked space in his house, the man had to sleep in the shack.

Around midnight the farmer was awakened by the delivery

man. He was shaking all over. "The place is haunted," the man swore, and went on to tell a frightening story.[3] It seems he had locked up the house and prepared for an early night's sleep in the small upstairs bedroom when he heard either the front or back door open. Someone, he claimed, came in, climbed the stairs, dropped his boots in the bedroom, and almost immediately fell asleep, snoring loudly. After searching the place from one end to the other, the man maintained, he could see no one in the house.

The man would have no more to do with that haunted shack. He packed his bag and left for Vancouver, leaving the farmer to learn to drive as best he could.

There is a possible explanation for the snoring. When someone is close to death, it is not uncommon for his or her breathing to become laboured. The condition is called "rales" and it can sound just like somebody snoring. The "snoring" then could be simply an at-the-time-of-death incident which for some reason was played back like a tape recorder in the small bedroom for years after the actual occurrence.

A Family of Ghosts

When it was built, the old house was probably one of Victoria's finest, but when John West bought it in 1969, it had fallen into disrepair. While the house had been empty, vandals had broken doors, smashed windows and removed most of the antique doorknobs. The grass in the front yard was knee deep and the trees around the property desperately needed pruning.

However, the large house had obviously been magnificent in its day. The two fireplaces, one in the living room and the other in the dining room, were still bordered by beautiful mantels of carved solid oak. Mr. West estimated it had been built around the turn of the century. It would be the kind of place to which former residents could become very attached — even to the point of staying on beyond the grave. At least that's what the tenants who moved in firmly believed. They were convinced that the house was haunted, and not by a single entity, but by a whole family of ghosts which even included an invisible cat. Within weeks of moving in, the people who shared the old house were severely frightened by the ghostly goings-on.

The house was rented in September 1969 to a young couple from Ontario, Brent and Jan Lowell (not their real names), who in turn took in several boarders, Gilles from Montreal and Bob from New York. In addition, an area upstairs was rented as a day studio by a young artist. All the tenants believed that the house was haunted by very active ghosts. "There's an old man," Jan Lowell began. "We believe him to be an old man by the way he walks. . . . He lives upstairs in the front room. He walks halfway down the stairs, stops and then goes back to his room."[4]

There were other ghosts as well. The woman and the baby were particularly chilling because people don't usually think of ghosts as being mothers with infants. "We can hear the baby cry," Jan continued. "The woman talks, but we've never been able to make out any words. It is as if she is comforting the baby."

Then there were the cat stories. Bob related one incident concerning a cat that no one could see:

> We were in the front living room when the cat came down. We could hear it padding down the stairs. It stopped at the hallway door, let out a meow. Then there seemed to be footsteps across the living room and it jumped on the fireplace mantel and began to meow again. [Three] of us were in the same room, but [we] couldn't see anything.

Immediately all three decided it was time to leave the room. The cat had also been heard scratching on the kitchen window, apparently to be let in. "I didn't believe in ghosts," Bob admitted, "not until I moved into this house."

On another occasion Bob and five friends entered the kitchen to find broken glass covering the floor. They were just going to clean up the mess when suddenly they were aware of the sound

of someone walking close by. The footsteps, Bob noted, "...
came into the kitchen, made a terrible racket. It also sounded as
if someone dropped a broom." Bob and his visitors made a
hasty exit from the kitchen.

Most of those living in the house watched various doors open
and shut without human assistance. "Someone might say it is
because the house is settling," Brent observed. "But look at the
house. It's built on a rock, with a rock and cement foundation."

The tenants were not alone in what they felt about the house.
Brent claimed that once their sceptical friends had had an op-
portunity to experience the house, "Every one changed his
view." Even John West, the owner, had a feeling that there was
something creepy about the place. While renovating the structure, he became aware of one room with a cold drafty spot,
where there was no place for air to get in.

The fact that the presences seemed more palpable during the
daytime, when the owner was working on the house, makes this
haunting a little different from most cases. Usually, unexplained phenomena occur during the night. These ghosts,
however, exhibited a marked preference for the afternoon, and
were never felt or heard during the evening or night hours.

Unlike other tenants who had quickly moved on, the young
couple and their boarders stayed, even in the face of the strange
happenings in the house. It was Bob's opinion that a person
could adjust to almost anything. "It's weird," he noted, "I feel
safe and secure most of the time. Then, at times when I'm
alone, I get the feeling that I'm not supposed to be there. I drop
whatever I'm doing and walk out."

It has been 20 years since the ghosts frightened the young
tenants of the old Victoria house. While the exact location of
the house was not mentioned at the time the haunting was reported, several Victoria ghost sleuths say they think it stood on
Quadra Street. If they are right, the house was torn down some
time ago to make way for a church.

* * * * *

Interestingly, there is another apparently haunted house in Victoria which has recently met the wrecker's ball. This house, built around the turn of the century, was an eerie old place completely surrounded by thorn bushes. The bushes made everything more spooky because they seemed to be constantly scratching against the sides of the house — even when it wasn't windy.

In 1977, when Rick Johnston moved into the old house on Vernon Street, the former tenants, who were moving out the last of their belongings, yelled, "Take good care of our friend."[5] He, of course, didn't know what they meant, but he soon found out.

Johnston had not been in the house long when one night he and a friend were sitting in the living room. Suddenly an ashtray which had been on one end of the coffee table slid the entire length of the table and fell to the floor. Neither man was anywhere near the ashtray at the time. Another strange occurrence concerned Johnston's bedroom door. It was his habit to close his door when he retired for the night. However, after living in the house about two weeks he began to notice that when he got up in the morning, the door would be open.

Whatever was haunting the old house seemed to take particular pleasure in playing with the old ringer washer in the basement. "I'd be sitting there at night and I'd listen and it would be on," he recalled. "I would go down and turn it off and un-plug it. But when I got up in the morning it would be on again."

There were other incidents as well. The ghost apparently liked heat. When Johnston returned from work the thermostat would frequently be turned " . . . up as high as it would go." Johnston found the incidents so unsettling he finally moved out of the house. Not long afterwards, the house was torn down to make way for a new supermarket.

A Creepy Old Haunt

Like Victoria, the old city of New Westminster on the mainland seems to have a large number of ghosts. One apparently
well-haunted residence is the house owned by Jim and Lou
Dodds. It is a huge, 13-room structure, built almost a hundred
years ago, when New Westminster was still the major city on
the mainland and Vancouver only a young upstart. When the
Dodds moved in in 1967, the house had long fallen on hard
times and was in need of considerable repair. Dodds, a carpen-
ter, spent much of his free time renovating it.

The Dodds had been living in the house about two years
when the first incident happened. A family friend who was staying with them was sleeping in one of the bedrooms, when he
awoke to catch, out of the corner of his eye, the image of a man
in the room with him. The figure was standing by the window
staring off into the night. The man seemed middle aged, but
the clothes he was wearing were all wrong. The hat and long
coat were clearly from an earlier time.

When the friend turned his head to gain a better look at the
stranger, the figure immediately vanished. The Dodds's guest
was apparently not the only one who witnessed the spectre.
Raggs, the family dog, was found some time later hiding
beneath the bed. The unfortunate pet had clearly seen something that frightened it very much.

Dodds also had a strange experience one night, when he
checked the house before retiring for bed. Everything on the
ground floor seemed perfectly normal, so he switched off the
lights and turned toward the staircase. When he reached the
foot of the stairs, he put his hand on the newel post. Suddenly
he was aware of a strange sensation. He felt as though someone
in the darkness had taken his hand. When he moved up the
stairs the mysterious hand-holder continued to accompany him.
"I didn't know what to think," he said later. "I wasn't scared,
but [the feeling] was very real."[6] Finally, he was forced to shake
his hand free.

At night, when Mrs. Dodds was up late working around the

59

house, she felt a presence, "like a whirlwind around me," and the room she was in suddenly felt icy cold. Mrs. Dodds also saw, on the stairs, what she described as "the shadow of a woman... wearing a long dress."

There was also the light switch in the upstairs bathroom. The switch, Dodds explained, was one of the old-fashioned spring-loaded types: it took considerable force to turn it off or on. Sometimes however, when the entire family was downstairs, the sound of that upstairs switch clicking on and off would be heard.

Following the death of his wife in September 1988, Dodds continued to note strange goings-on in the house. Once, after he had retired for the night, he saw a white smokey shape appear just above his bed. The wispy form, he recalled later, "seemed to give off a faint glow."[7] At first he was frightened, but then it occurred to him that there was nothing in the house to harm him. He turned over and went to sleep.

* * * * *

It is interesting to note that in the two houses discussed in this chapter, considerable repairs were being undertaken. Some psychical investigators have postulated that physical changes to a dwelling bring about paranormal occurrences. One classic case comes from England. When a fire escape was added to a Northamptonshire inn quite recently, the resident ghost, said to be Queen Mary of Scotland, appeared to three different occupants of the "haunted room" on three successive nights.

Other strange events have been reported not far from London, England, where half a wall, the wainscotting for example, along the lower half of a hallway, has been removed. The resident ghost has reappeared sure enough, but the lower half of him — the half opposite the new wall — is missing.

Footsteps

In 1960, the Hilton family rented an unusual old house in White Rock. It came with the sound of distinctive footsteps creeping around the upstairs of the house. There was never anyone to be seen, but there was certainly something to be heard, and the family found these strange happenings, at the least, disturbing.

The footsteps had been heard by those outside the immediate family as well. Henry Hilton explained that over one Easter weekend his brother, Markland, and his wife visited them from Saskatchewan. This was not Hilton's brother's first visit to the White Rock house — he and his wife had been there three times before. Previously he had scoffed at the stories of the phantom footsteps but during this particular visit, the couple spent the night in one of the upstairs bedrooms.

The next morning, when Markland Hilton came downstairs, he looked pale and shaken. He stated that some time after midnight, he suddenly awoke to hear the sound of footsteps: someone was shuffling along the hallway just outside his bedroom. Then the footsteps seemed to turn into the room he and his wife were occupying. Markland asked who was there but he received no answer. The footsteps just kept on coming slowly. By then Markland was quite distressed. Although not a particularly religious man, he felt compelled to challenge the approaching steps "In the name of the Father, Son, and Holy Ghost."[8] Only then did the sound suddenly halt. Markland's wife heard the frightening noise as well and from then on she refused to go to the upstairs rooms unless someone went with her.

There might be several explanations for the strange noises. The Hiltons are a large family. (At the time when the sounds were reported in the press in 1963, Henry and Mary Hilton had eight children ranging in age from an infant to 18 years old.) Could the sounds have been made by one of the children? Not according to Mrs. Hilton who heard the footsteps in the afternoon when she was alone in the house. When the noises were heard members of the family would do quick checks of the

61

house, but nothing was ever discovered that would account for the sounds.

The house was also inspected thoroughly for possible causes of the phenomena. Tree branches striking the roof were ruled out and so were loose electric or telephone wires. Even more striking evidence against the "natural cause theory," was the fact that the noises sounded so clearly like shuffling footsteps. The Hiltons had lived in the house long enough to tell the difference between natural and unnatural noises in the house, and as far as they were concerned it was clear that the footsteps defied simple explanation.

As often happens, Mr. and Mrs. Hilton became used to the noises during the three years they lived at the White Rock house. After all, whatever it was never did anyone any harm. However, some of the younger children never became accustomed to the strange goings-on, and one little boy refused to go upstairs by himself.

The Rapping Ghost

Ghosts usually confine themselves to one house at a time, but on the odd occasion they have been known to haunt more than one location. This is the case in the small community of Wells, not far from Barkerville. Unlike Barkerville, Wells is comparatively new, owing its existence to a rich gold strike there in 1932.

In Wells there is a house owned by Ron Candy. On the surface there is nothing particularly unusual about the house: like most of the others on the same block, it was built some time in the early 1930s. During the 12 years Candy lived in the house, he experienced a number of odd incidents. The most common phenomenon involved rapping — usually three definite knocks — on the roof or back wall of his house. The sound is quite distinct: on one occasion a guest staying in the house woke Candy in the middle of the night, convinced that someone was trying to break in.

There were other unusual occurrences as well. In winter, particularly, perfume has been frequently noted just outside Candy's house. Those experiencing the scent have said that it occurs only in a clearly defined location. "You'd be walking along," Ron Candy recalled, "and you'd walk into this column of very pungent perfume. You could walk in and out of it... and you wouldn't smell it anywhere else." [9] It is unlikely that the perfume could have been carried on the wind from some other location: the column containing the scent was no more than a foot across.

However, the focus of these weird episodes has been not only Candy's residence: a number have taken place at a neighbouring dwelling, a log house until recently occupied by the Keeley family (not their real name). Although Candy's nearest neighbours were the Keeleys, their house was built on the opposite side of a cul-de-sac. During the time they lived in the cabin the Keeleys also heard rapping noises, apparently coming from the roof, and the ghost of a woman was apparently witnessed by at least one family member. The Keeleys have subsequently moved away from the log house and new occupants have moved in, but the mysterious rapping sound still continues. (The spectre, however, has not been seen again.) The Keeley house, although of quite recent construction, was built on the foundation of an old cabin that apparently predated the town of Wells, but unfortunately nothing more is known about the old cabin or its former occupants.

PART II: HAUNTED PLACES

The Phantom of
the Burn Unit

During the time of the Burn Unit haunting, the Vancouver General Hospital ordered its staff not to discuss the strange incidents with anyone outside the hospital. Hospital authorities quite rightly feared that publicity would disrupt the functioning of the unit. The public is fascinated by buildings supposedly inhabited by ghosts, and one can imagine crowds of ghost seekers interrupting the vital work of the nurses and doctors.

However, now that the building which housed the old Burn Unit has been demolished, and a new, ghost-free facility has been opened in its place, hospital authorities have allowed the nurses to speak out. It has been years since the episodes involving the young patient began, and most of the staff at the time have moved on to other hospitals; still, there are nurses working there who recall the events which occurred after the tragic death of one burn victim.

* * * * *

Nursing is a very demanding profession. Even in the midst of crisis the nurse is expected to carry on coolly and efficiently. From their first days in training, student nurses are taught observational skills: to see, hear, feel and touch. Thus, when the incidents began in the Burn Unit in early 1976, they were witnessed by thoroughly professional observers. There was no question in the minds of many of the nurses working there that the Burn Unit was haunted.

People who work in large grain-storage facilities are aware that grain dust is a highly explosive substance. Over the years there have been many grain elevator explosions in other parts of the continent, but workers at Burrard Terminals Ltd. in North Vancouver felt they were less at risk than their prairie counterparts. The damp British Columbia climate, it was believed, moistened the grain and made it less volatile. The fallacy of this idea was tragically demonstrated on October 3, 1975, when a small fire in a conveyor belt touched off a massive explosion that killed one man instantly and sent 16 others to hospital. Those suffering serious burns were sent to the Burn Unit.

One of the victims in critical condition was 28-year-old Douglas Woods (not his real name). As nurses and doctors examined the young man it was clear that the prognosis was not good. Victims of severe burns often cling to life for a few days, weeks or even months before finally succumbing to their injuries, suffering terrible pain before eventually being released by death.

As the staff working in the intensive care area soon discovered, Douglas was no ordinary patient: he had an incredible will to live. Even though he faced tremendous pain, he fought on. Aided by a warm family and many close friends, he continued to beat the odds, yet, slowly, the pain of his terrible ordeal sapped the young man's strength.

Just before his death, Douglas confided that he was sure he was going to die. "I'm very tired," he told a nurse, "and I've had so much pain."[1] The nurse who was with him was surprised because in the three months he'd been on the ward he'd come so far. She tried to give him some encouragement, but he seemed quite resigned to his fate. The next day Douglas's heart suddenly stopped.

Unit staff found it difficult to accept Douglas's sudden passing. His tenacity in the face of incredible pain had been inspiring. However, the young man made it plain that he was not really very far away. Soon after his death, a relief night nurse from another ward went into 415, Douglas's old room. She looked in the direction of what had been his bed to see the covers suddenly shift, just as if someone had rolled over. There was also a noise coming from that direction, the soft rhythmical sound of breathing, but nobody had been admitted to Douglas's bed.

Not long after the first incident, there were others. One of the other nurses who has since left reported entering 415, which was unoccupied, and being unable to shake a very powerful feeling that someone was in the room with her. The two-bed room was used for intensive-care patients and between the beds there was a sink. The nurse's eyes moved around until her gaze reached the area between the beds. In front of the sink she watched a vague shape move slowly around the end of the bed and out through the door.

On another occasion, a male nurse, Denny Conrad, and another nurse were quickly readying room 413 for a new admission. Conrad was preoccupied with preparations, so as he came into the room with a load of laundry bags, he was barely aware of his colleague's white form standing with a dressing tray. As Conrad turned to speak to the other person in the room, the dressings fell to the floor. "It wasn't her at all, it was [Douglas]."[2] Conrad abruptly turned and left the room. In retrospect it seems clear that Douglas was only trying to help prepare the dressing for the patient, but nurses, like almost everyone else, have difficulty dealing with ghosts, and Conrad was severely shaken by the incident.

It was not only staff members who saw Douglas. A nurse reported an incident involving a woman who was admitted with terrible burns. It was obvious that she had only a short time to live and all the staff could do was to make her as comfortable as possible. As a new shift came on the nurse entered the room to check on the patient. The patient looked up and said, "Oh by the way there was a strange young man just in here visiting me."

The nurse was shocked that anyone outside the woman's immediate family could have visited this critically ill patient.

"Who did you say was here?" she asked.

"He said his name was [Douglas]," came the patient's reply.[3]

On another occasion, nurse Alice Bishop (not her real name) recalled making rounds with other ward staff one morning. A man who had been badly burned was placed in room 413, next to Douglas's former room. She spoke with the patient for a moment before he suddenly said, "I'd like to thank that young doctor who took the time last night to come in and help me with the pain."[4]

All the staff in the room were surprised, but no one said anything until they were outside the patient's door. They questioned each other about who the patient could possibly mean; there should have been no doctor on the ward the previous evening. Finally a nurse phoned the night shift staff, now off duty, and confirmed that indeed no doctor had visited the ward. Much perplexed, one staff member went back into the patient's room and asked him to recall the person who had been in to see him last night. The description fit only one person: it was Douglas.

"The nurses on the floor," Ms. Bishop later acknowledged, "never told the patient that the young man who had been so helpful was a ghost."

Douglas seemed to have two missions on the ward. The first was to ease the suffering of other patients. This was not surprising to the staff; after all, he had suffered considerable pain for a long time. It seemed only logical, knowing Douglas, that he would try to make the pain easier for other burn victims. Douglas's second mission, it seems, was to announce to the staff that he was still very definitely in the Burn Unit. It was the way Douglas chose to announce this fact that caused so much difficulty with the nurses.

As Conrad recalled, "Other night shifts that I worked there — especially night shifts — you'd be walking by and the radio would be full blast all of a sudden. The toilet would flush, or you'd be sitting at the nursing station and the [call] light for 415 would go on." Of course, the room would be unoccupied at the time.[5]

Ms. Bishop related an incident concerning a nurse who had gone into Douglas's former room to hang a bottle of intravenous solution. "Suddenly she felt strange, and then very cold, like she was covered in ice. Displaying remarkable courage she said in an even voice, 'Look [Douglas], I know you're here, but I'm really busy tonight, so please don't interrupt me.' Then suddenly the coldness lifted and she was able to go on about her work."[6]

For a time the strange occurrences were so common that most of the staff simply tried to adjust to the situation. Room 415 was the centre of the paranormal activity and nurses frequently would take only ten-minute shifts in that room. The intense cold, the strange prickly feeling in the scalp, taps turning, toilets flushing, and lights going on and off — it was too much for them. They couldn't take it for long. As Conrad recalled later, "I'd walk in there and [my] hair would stand right up. And you knew he was there. It was just awful."[7]

However, although the haunting put the staff under considerable tension, there was never any feeling of evil. The staff were convinced that Douglas simply wanted to make sure everyone knew he was not far away. As time passed, the disturbances decreased, yet it was only when the staff moved to a new facility and the old building was torn down that the haunting stopped completely.

If there is a lesson to be drawn from the Burn Unit haunting it is that ghosts cannot exist on the same plane with living human beings, at least not without causing considerable difficulty. Douglas was a warm and caring person who wished only to relieve the suffering of others who, like himself, faced acute distress, but his presence made it very difficult for the Burn Unit to operate properly. It is not Douglas's fault, of course. People find it hard to overcome their fear of ghosts, even when, like Douglas, the ghosts have the best of intentions.

Haunted Schools

Beyond the fact that both facilities have served as educational institutions, the old Craigflower School and Royal Roads Military College would appear to have little in common. Craigflower is very old, dating back to the middle of the last century. Royal Roads, on the other hand, has been an educational establishment only since the Second World War. However, they share one feature that makes them different from other schools in the province: both are haunted.

The Old Craigflower School

There are a number of frightening stories relating to the old Craigflower school building in Saanich on Vancouver Island. The origin of the following tale is not known, so its authenticity must be suspect. It has been suggested that a summary of this particular incident may have been given by the long-time school caretaker, Hugh Palliser, to the archives in Victoria, but if so there is no record of it, today.

*　*　*　*　*

The first Craigflower School was completed in 1855 by Vancouver Island's colonial administration for the children of Hudson's Bay Company employees and other settlers who had established farms in the area. The school was on Victoria's Portage Inlet in a spot that was conveniently reached by boat and horse, but because many farms were isolated it was necessary for some of the students to board in. Living quarters for the teacher and students were thus included in the school plan. Craigflower School was a tribute to the increasing self-reliance of the early settlers; wood for construction came from the Hudson's Bay Company's own steam-powered sawmill on Craigflower Farm, not far from the school, and the bricks used for the foundation were manufactured in a local kiln.

The wreck of the 150-ton ship, *Major Tompkins*, in 1855 provided Craigflower with one important school fixture. While the ship was eventually battered to pieces on the rocks off Esquimalt, all the passengers and crew escaped with their lives; there was even time to save the ship's bell which was duly presented to the school. From then on, the bell off the old *Major Tompkins* dutifully called students to class at Craigflower.

The old school served until 1911, when a new structure was completed nearby. After the new facility was complete, the living quarters in the old school were retained as a residence for the school's caretaker. It was when caretaker Hugh Palliser and his family were occupying the residence that the haunting first came about.

One day in early September 1918, the rotting old Craigflower bridge collapsed, taking with it a big gravel truck. While the driver escaped unhurt, the truck was partially submerged in about ten feet of water. The old bridge adjoined the Craigflower School grounds; thus, when operations to salvage the truck began, it was necessary to attach a heavy anchor line to school property so that the truck could be winched up the gorge.

Palliser stood in the school yard watching the operation. The job went well enough until workmen began clearing away brush and debris from the site selected for anchoring the winch line. One of the men gave a yell as his shovel turned something over. It wasn't much, just a few small bones. Thinking that it was only the remains of some small animal the man went back

Craigflower School. (COURTESY OF BC ARCHIVES)

to work.

It wasn't long, however, before he again stopped suddenly. This time the blade of his shovel had turned over something that was quite unmistakable. Clearly exposed in the hole were a number of long thin bones. The caretaker could easily identify them as the bones of a human arm. The man dug carefully now, and soon a human skull was exposed. Palliser took it from the shallow excavation and began brushing off the heavy clay soil that clung to it. It was yellowed with age, and many of the teeth were missing. Digging further in the hole the men found a complete human skeleton. Like the skull, all the bones were very brown and old-looking.

Hugh Palliser walked back to the school, returning a few minutes later with a large wooden box. The caretaker and the workmen gathered the bones and placed them in the box. As far as the caretaker was concerned, it was obvious what had happened. The workmen had accidentally disturbed the ancient grave of an Indian.

"My youngest daughter is studying anatomy," he told the workmen. "We'll let her have a look at these and put them [together]." [1] When they had recovered everything Palliser closed the lid tightly. The men returned to the task of anchoring the support cable while Palliser picked up the box and carried it to the woodshed which adjoined the old school building. He put the box on one of the long shelves which lined the walls of the shed and then returned to his own tasks around the school.

After supper that evening, Palliser and his wife settled around the kitchen stove to read. It was unusually cold for early September, but the schoolhouse was nevertheless quite comfortable. Then the quiet of the evening was suddenly broken by a sharp click. It was the sound made by the latch being raised on the door leading from the kitchen to the woodshed. Both Mr. and Mrs. Palliser put down their books and waited for someone to come in through the kitchen door. The door was a crude affair consisting of five or six boards laid edge to edge, and held together by several crosspieces. The door stayed shut by means of an ordinary thumb latch. The mechanism was quite simple, but once the latch was shut it could not be lifted without applying considerable pressure. As the Pallisers watched, the door swung open, but nothing came in except a cold blast of air.

Palliser got up and walked through the woodshed to the outside door, but to his surprise it was closed tightly. "Funny," he said to himself. "I'd have sworn the outside door was open by the way the wind came in." Returning to the kitchen, he securely closed the door to the woodshed.

The family passed the remainder of the evening quietly. As they were preparing for bed, however, the caretaker again heard the distinctive click of the door latch being opened. He returned to the kitchen to investigate. Once more as he watched, the door to the shed swung open. Again a cold blast of air poured out from the inky blackness of the shed. Palliser took a lantern and returned to the woodshed, but the outside door was still bolted shut. The cold wind seemed to arise out of nowhere.

In the lantern light he examined the woodshed. There was no hole in the roof of the shed. There was no gap along the outside walls. No space had suddenly opened up to let the elements in. Wood for the stove was stacked neatly in a pile on the floor, while on the walls his tools were properly hung in place. Along one wall, his wife's preserves filled the shelves, and along another were household odds and ends the family had stored. Nothing was out of order.

Palliser was just about to return to the kitchen when the light from the lantern fell on the wooden box he had placed there earlier in the day. He pulled the lid off the box. There in the pale light the caretaker could see the ancient yellow skull grinning up at him. As he looked on, the lantern light flickered wildly, making the shadows dance. It was as if the bones had come to life. He quickly returned the lid to the box and left.

In the kitchen, he again securely fastened the door to the woodshed before retiring himself. There was no further disturbance that night, but the following evening Palliser was ready for whoever, or as he feared, whatever, was behind the door to the woodshed. After his wife and children had retired early to bed, the caretaker sat alone in the kitchen reading the paper and waiting. His chair was placed only inches from the door, and on the floor next to him was a lantern.

It was quite late when he heard the noise again: the unmistakable click of the latch. Immediately Palliser looked up, and as he watched dumbfounded the latch slowly lifted and stopped in the up position. Quickly grabbing his lantern, he closed his hand on the latch handle, then flung the door open.

Hugh Palliser was a down-to-earth Yorkshireman, certainly not the kind of individual to give way to wild flights of fancy. He had often heard the wind whistle through the old schoolhouse on lonely winter nights, and knew it for what it was. He also knew that what he had seen and heard these last two nights was no figment of his imagination and that when the lantern light filled the black space behind the door, he would be staring at whatever had moved the mechanism of the latch. The flickering light played across the woodshed to reveal nothing but that same icy blast of wind. Palliser walked through the woodshed to the outside door. It was just as he left it earlier that evening: bolted shut from the inside. No living being could have got in there.

Next he took the box from the shelf and opened it. There in the dim light, the skull looked up at him; now though, the grin seemed evil. The caretaker knew what he had to do. He took a spade from among the tools in the shed, and opened the outside door. With his lantern in one hand, and his spade and the box of bones under his arm, Palliser walked out into the pitch-black night.

Somewhere in the school yard Hugh Palliser dug a new grave for the yellowed bones. When the hole was deep enough he took the box and placed it in the grave. Even years later, he never revealed exactly where the ancient bones were buried, but his assumption had been correct: with the last spadeful of earth spread over the yellowed bones, this particular haunting of the old Craigflower School came abruptly to an end.

* * * * *

The Craigflower schoolhouse is the oldest school building still surviving in western Canada. It is currently operated as a heritage museum by the provincial government. The old school has been the site of many strange goings-on, and those closely associated with the museum over the years have reported many unusual happenings.

C. J. (Jerry) Clark will not forget the period between 1970 and 1980 when he acted as live-in caretaker at the Craigflower School museum. One night Clark was sitting at a table in the school answering some letters. His dog, Dixie, was lying on the floor beside him. Suddenly the dog began to growl. Clark put his pen down and listened closely. There were voices coming from the other side of the wall in the area of the washroom.

Clark checked the room but could find nothing to account for the sounds. He then expanded his search to include the entire building, but there was no sign of intruders either inside or outside the building. "There was no sign of anybody around anywhere." [2]

There were other occasions when unexplained noises were heard. Once, just after the last visitor had left, Clark and his wife, who had been acting as tour guides, stopped outside for a break. Suddenly there was a tremendous banging and clatter somewhere in the school. When the Clarks arrived to investigate, the noise stopped abruptly. Again, there were no intruders to be found anywhere on Craigflower School property.

At other times the school bell from the old *Major Tompkins* would suddenly start ringing on its own. Then, adding to the cacophony, other school bells would join in until the building shook with the sound. "We thought it was vandals — kids running around — but there was not a thing," Clark recalled. "What started the bells to suddenly ring always was a mystery."

On one occasion Clark heard what sounded like someone dragging a chain down a set of stairs which led to the top floor. Again there was nothing the caretaker could see that would explain these noises.

What could account for the Craigflower School phenomena? One explanation may be that a number of ancient remains had been disturbed there. Apparently the Craigflower School property included part of a large Indian burial ground. An article in the Victoria *Daily Times* for December 20, 1911, noted that while contractors were excavating the construction of the new Craigflower School (across the street from the old one), they came across five skulls buried with a number of arrow heads. It is conceivable that there are yet other restless spirits in the vicinity of the old school.

Royal Roads Military College

In the best tradition of other military academies, including West Point in the United States, Royal Roads Military College, not far from Victoria, has its own ghost. The Royal Roads ghost has been seen many times by the cadets in residence there, but unfortunately none of these incidents have been documented, and with the rapid turnover of students attending the school, the accounts have tended to be taken away with each graduating class. As far as can be determined, the Royal Roads haunting predates 1940, when the college was established. Before the building was purchased by the defence department, it had been the home of the James Dunsmuir family.

James Dunsmuir, the son of the Vancouver Island coal baron, Robert Dunsmuir, played an important role in the political life of this province. During the first decade of this century, he served first as premier, then as lieutenant-governor, though politics, generally, were not to the taste of this very reserved man. When he resigned as premier on November 21, 1902, he had filled the position for less than three years. In 1906 he was appointed to the largely ceremonial office of lieutenant-governor. He retired from public life in 1909, and died in 1920.

During his time as lieutenant-governor, while the family lived at Government House, Dunsmuir decided to construct a residence befitting his exalted social station. Earlier, in 1892, three years after the death of his father, he had built a home for himself and his family on the banks of Victoria's Gorge. Burleith, as it was called, was an attractive mansion, but quite modest — at least in terms of Craigdarroch Castle, James's mother's palatial residence in Victoria.

The new Dunsmuir mansion was a huge, Norman-styled affair with 600 acres of formal gardens and treed parkland. Hatley Park, as the Dunsmuirs called their new home, was lavish in the extreme. "Money doesn't matter," James Dunsmuir was reported to have told the contractors. "Just build what I want." The result was arguably the most beautiful private residence in the province, surpassing even Craigdarroch.

The building was huge: there were a dozen bedrooms and nine bathrooms in the main wing alone. Extra features included a third-floor ballroom which could be reached by elevator. When it was finally completed in 1908, the Dunsmuirs' new home had cost an estimated $4,000,000, and the expenses didn't stop there: a staff of a hundred was needed just to maintain the mansion, gardens, and six miles of roads on the property. After the completion of Hatley Park, Laura Dunsmuir, James's wife, and her daughters gave many magnificent parties there. Attending such galas were not only the local celebrities, but also many important members of the British aristocracy. James Dunsmuir, however, was becoming more and more a recluse — he shunned these social events.

In 1929, nine years after the death of James Dunsmuir, the New York stock market crashed, and much of Laura Dunsmuir's wealth was wiped out virtually overnight. It is not difficult to imagine how Mrs. Dunsmuir, a member of what until

Hatley Park, now Royal Roads, ca *1912.* (COURTESY OF BC ARCHIVES)

recently had been British Columbia's most important family, suffered during this period. She had lost almost everything. She attempted to meet at least some of the cost of maintaining Hatley Park by opening the gardens to the public for a fee, but during the depression, few people could afford the luxury of a garden visit. Stories began to circulate in Victoria that Laura Dunsmuir was almost destitute; that creditors held off foreclosing on the property only because the elderly woman was so ill.

Mrs. Dunsmuir passed away in 1937 and Hatley Park remained empty for almost four years. A small staff was retained to maintain the property. Soon after Mrs. Dunsmuir's death one of the maids reported that she felt uncomfortable there — as though someone unseen was watching her as she went about her work. The feeling was so intense that she was reluctant to go into some of the rooms alone.

In 1940 the estate was purchased by the defence department for $75,000 — less than the original cost of the stone fence which surrounds the property. The following year Hatley Park was turned into a school to train naval officers, who, because of the war, were in short supply. The fact that the building was now the property of the navy did nothing to lessen its increasingly eerie reputation. Students working late at night claimed to be suddenly overcome by a strange feeling — like coming into contact with a mass of freezing cobwebs. This feeling usually occurred on the second and third floors of the building.

Although details are scarce, students have admitted seeing the apparition of a little old woman standing by their beds. A Royal Roads Public Information Officer, Captain Martin Marshall, recalls one incident about ten years ago when he was still a cadet at the institution.

A cadet who was acting as senior duty officer appeared one morning quite pale and shaken and told a most unusual tale. He had fallen asleep the previous night as usual, but some time in the early hours of the morning he was awakened by someone pulling his leg. As he opened his eyes he saw the apparition of a woman before him. He tried to shake his leg from her grip but the spectre held on. As strong as the young cadet was, it took considerable effort to break free, but once he did manage to loosen her hold, the spectre disappeared.

It is perhaps not surprising that the spirit of the mistress of Hatley Park would return to her home; during the last years of her life the fate of the family mansion was probably very much on her mind. Moreover, it is possible to imagine what she might think to see so many young men occupying Hatley Park. The ghost's reaction may have indeed been to shake one cadet awake, and drag him from *her* house. However, there may be more than one ghost in residence. A psychic who visited Hatley Park some years ago stated that there may have been a second presence there. She believed that Mrs. Dunsmuir's daughter, Eleanor, who died shortly after her mother, also haunted the family estate.

* * * * *

There is another brief Dunsmuir ghost story that may be mentioned here. James Dunsmuir's brother Alex, who lived in San Francisco, had a long history of alcohol abuse. Despite his wife Josephine's best efforts to keep him straight, Alex Dunsmuir continued drinking to excess, and by 1899, it was clear that his health was failing rapidly.

Dunsmuir's poor health was of course a considerable worry to his wife, but during the final months of his illness she had her own concern. She had been feeling unwell for some time and when she visited her doctor his diagnosis was most distressing — cancer. She was advised to have an operation as soon as possible, but because her husband was so ill, Mrs. Dunsmuir put off the ordeal. Alex Dunsmuir died on January 31, 1899, in New York.

Following the funeral, which was held in San Francisco, Mrs. Dunsmuir decided to postpone the operation for a little longer. She agreed to spend a few weeks with her brother-in-law, James Dunsmuir, and his family in Victoria. The Dunsmuirs were at the time still living at Burleith, their mansion overlooking the Gorge.

One day while standing by her bedroom window, the grieving widow was suddenly surprised to see the apparition of her late husband beside her. The ghost looked at her and said, "Josephine, pet, you'd better not stay too long or you'll be late for your operation."[3] Mrs. Dunsmuir quickly packed her bags and left for San Francisco where she underwent the operation.

The ghost, it seems, had no special prescient abilities. Even after the operation Josephine Dunsmuir's health continued to decline, and she died the following year.

The Phantom of the Links

She has been given many names over the years — the Watcher, the April Ghost, the Oak Bay Ghost, or the Ghost of Golf Course Point. After a quiet period in the 1970s when there were few sightings, Victoria's most sought-after ghost has again become active. On moon-lit spring nights local high school and university students continue to make an annual pilgrimage to the Victoria Golf Club where they hope to see the elusive spectre for themselves. It is not surprising that this beautiful lady in the diaphanous wedding dress has such a special appeal to young people, for as legend has it she is, literally, their ghost. According to local folk tales, this particular apparition is seen only by young couples, but there's a catch: this is not a spot to take your true love, for the tale also says that couples seeing the ghost will never marry.

Actually, there is little romance associated with the story of Doris Gravlin, the young woman who is thought to haunt the Victoria Golf Course; her death was simply a senseless waste. The young and attractive auburn-haired nurse was liked by almost everyone, but in September 1936, she was having difficulty with her estranged husband, Victor. Victor was sports editor at one of Victoria's daily newspapers, but he had developed a severe drinking problem. In the late summer of 1936, Doris had been separated from him for almost two years.

After leaving her husband, Mrs. Gravlin was hired as a private nurse by Mrs. Kathleen Richardson, who lived in an apartment on Beach Drive in Oak Bay. Mrs. Richardson later testified before an inquest that Mrs. Gravlin left about eight o'clock on the evening of September 22, to go for a walk. She never returned.

Five days later a Victoria Golf Club caddy, John Johnson, was looking for a lost ball on the shoreline near the seventh tee, when he noticed a woman's sweater lying on the beach. As he bent to pick it up he saw Mrs. Gravlin's body in a patch of tall grass and bush.

The subsequent police investigation determined that the woman had been murdered in a patch of wild broom beside the seventh hole and her body dragged down to the beach. An autopsy revealed that she had been beaten and then strangled, probably by a piece of cord which was then used to drag the body to the beach. Strangely, the woman's white kid leather shoes, which she had been known to be wearing the night of her death, were missing and could not be found, even after a careful search of the vicinity of the murder.

The investigation soon turned up one interesting fact: Doris Gravlin's estranged husband, Victor, also disappeared the night of September 22. Gravlin, who had been living with his parents, told them about eight o'clock that evening that he was going out for a stroll. He never returned. After the inquest, the police issued a warrant for his arrest in connection with the murder of his wife.

Despite the best efforts of police, however, Gravlin could not be located. On October 25, exactly four weeks after the discovery of the remains of Mrs. Gravlin, her husband's body was found. A man rowing off the shore of the golf links saw Gravlin's body entangled in a bed of kelp. It was estimated he had been dead four weeks. In the inside pocket of his coat police found Mrs. Gravlin's missing shoes.

At that time the full story was never printed in the paper, but people who knew the couple were able to put a human face on the tragedy, and since many of them were employed by Victoria newspapers, the story slowly leaked into print. The picture that emerged was of two young people who were desperately in love.

There was only one problem, but it was enough to drive them apart — liquor turned Victor Gravlin from a typical "nice guy" into a monster. It wasn't that Victor didn't sincerely try to give up alcohol; in fact he attempted to quit repeatedly, but always without success. Even faced with the end of his marriage he could not stop.

The activities of the Golf Course Ghost have kept the 1936 murder in the news, and the story in the press recently says that on the day of the tragedy Victor phoned Doris and promised to give up whisky. She agreed to meet him that evening at one of their favourite spots — the Oak Bay Beach Hotel, not far from the Victoria Golf Course — so that they could talk about a possible reconciliation. After having tea at the hotel restaurant, the couple went for a walk on the golf course. Whether this was true or not is unclear, but it is known that at about nine o'clock that evening someone living not far from the golf course heard a terrible scream. Since Victor was not seen after his wife's death, it is believed that he drowned himself soon after he killed her.

With the discovery of Victor's body the police closed the official investigation into the murder of Doris Gravlin, but the unfortunate young woman was not about to be forgotten. Exactly when strange occurrences began in the area of Golf Course Point, is not known, but by the 1940s there were already tales of eerie happenings there after dark.

One of the earliest reports concerns an unnamed fisherman. One evening at dusk the man was casting a line from a rocky outcropping which jutted away from the shore beside the golf course. Later he couldn't say what drew his attention, but when he glanced toward the shore, he saw a young woman standing at the edge of the water, on the lee side of the point. She was quite close to him, no more than a couple of yards away, and he could see her quite clearly, even though the light was beginning to fail. She appeared real, but what struck him as odd was that she was wearing an old-fashioned brown suit (not the wedding dress which was to become identified with her later). Also he noted she wore a morose expression, and just stood there staring sadly out to sea.

He made a couple of casts while the young woman continued to stand there silently. "Then," he was later reported to have said, "she suddenly hurried down as if she was going to meet someone, and on the way, she vanished. I saw her kind of melt away."[1]

In early April 1964, there was an incident involving a 16-year-old, boy, Anthony Gregson, and his girlfriend (the girl asked not to be identified, although she corroborated the boy's story). About nine o'clock on that pleasant spring evening, Gregson and the girl were walking on the golf course near the small point of land that juts out into the bay. Both youngsters were familiar with the folk tales of the ghost, and they laughed and joked lightheartedly about the spectre. At first the young couple was not aware of anything unusual, but as Gregson later told reporters, inexplicably the atmosphere seemed to change. There was suddenly something very strange in the air, and they both became unusually serious. Then they saw a ghost.

Gregson was obviously shocked by the incident — he later described the apparition as an incredible thousand yards away — but he had no doubt about what he saw. He took the phantom to be a woman because it was wearing a dress. However, unlike the apparition seen by the fisherman, there was no chance this one could be mistaken for a living person. It was a sort of luminous gray in colour, and it was surrounded by an aura. "The ghost," according to young Gregson, "moved with much more ease than a human and a certain grace of action, especially in her arms. Other features were less distinct."[2]

She moved along the beach, but what he noticed as particularly strange was that her feet seemed to pass over the pebbles on the shore without coming into contact with them. As the couple watched, the ghostly shape continued along the edge of the water. When she finally reached the end of the point she stopped abruptly and gazed out over the water as if waiting expectantly for someone. "I would rather like to think she was," Gregson added.

When the couple finally turned to leave, the ghost was still there at the end of the point. The entire incident had taken at least five minutes, and both young people had seen the same thing. "I am certain of what I saw," Gregson recalled. "I returned to the golf course the next day and checked all the land formations to make sure I was not mistaken." He didn't seem to be the kind of person to make up such a story. A Grade 11 student at nearby Oak Bay High School, the boy was described by Principal John B. Wallace as a good student and certainly not a young man given to wild flights of imagination.

Almost anyone who comes face to face with an apparition finds it very frightening and young Anthony Gregson was no exception. "I believe in leaving ghosts to their own lives. I am not going back [to the golf course] again. It was an unnerving experience."

There were, of course, many other young people who were eager to search out the ghost of Golf Course Point. About the end of April 1968, 16-year-old Ann Smith was walking through the golf course with a group of school friends. Like Anthony Gregson, she noticed a sudden change in the atmosphere. It was about nine o'clock in the evening, when Smith became aware that something was happening: "There was no noise, but although it was a warm night, it began to get windy and cold near the sand pit. It was a clammy coldness."[3]

Then she saw a misty figure in the shape of a woman. It was less than five feet tall. Although the misty figure herself was not well defined, she stood out clearly from the background. There was no mist beyond the outline of the phantom.

Bravely the group decided to return to Golf Course Point the next night to see if they would encounter her again. The ghost appeared, looking much as she had the previous night. Sixteen-year-old Dennis Andrews noticed that the figure seemed to glow. "It was about five feet tall and moved in an upright position, but I couldn't distinguish many of its features, although it looked like a woman," he reported. "It definitely was not swamp gas," a young seaman who was with the group observed. "I know what that looks like."

As the group watched closely it became clear that the spectre was more substantial than they first supposed. "At first I thought I could see right through it," said one unidentified witness. "But after a while I realized it was opaque."

The apparition was observed by the group for about five minutes. Some of the braver members present that evening tried to get closer for a better look, but the eerie lady apparently had other ideas. "I started to walk toward her and she disappeared," Ann Smith said, "but then we turned around and she was behind us, about 20 feet away."

The late 1960s was a very active time for the Golf Course Point Ghost. A Toronto cab driver, George Drysdale, who was in Victoria during this period, accompanied his sister and some friends to Golf Course Point to see if they could find the ghost one evening. Drysdale, at the time, was sceptical, but he was in for a surprise. In the bright moonlight, he recalled, the group could see quite well. He was the first to see the apparition of a

Victoria Golf Course. (PHOTOGRAPH BY THE AUTHOR)

girl. Afraid, the young man turned from her, but whatever direction he faced she would suddenly appear. "She was young and looked quite human," he said, "except for the fact that the whole outline of her body was shadowy at the edges — a very creepy effect. She looked sad — my God how sad she looked!" [4]

Drysdale's companions watched, horrified, as he tried to get away from the spectre, but he couldn't. Wherever he went it appeared in front of him. By now the young man was exceedingly frightened, because the ghost had picked him to torment, and there was simply no way to escape. Then like a flash, she was gone.

There was no doubt in Drysdale's mind about what he had seen. "A human being cannot appear in different places in the twinkling of an eye and vanish the same way," he said. "I *know* I saw the ghost of the murdered girl."

In the 1970s, ghostly activity at Golf Course Point almost stopped. Alarmed by the absence of the lady, the Victoria *Daily Times* sent reporter Al Forrest and photographer John MacKay to investigate. Many experts on the phantom wouldn't have thought the pair had a chance of seeing anything. Most sightings were reported in early spring; this was the middle of June. The ghost was usually seen about dusk; the two men arrived at eleven PM. However, Forrest believed he saw something strange there that night. "It was a white shape, swirling in the tall grass about 15 metres from the beach," the reporter observed. [5] By the time he could train his binoculars on it, it had vanished.

A few minutes later Forrest noted a rapid change in the atmosphere where they were standing. "Suddenly it got very cold; there was a chill that cut right through me." Forrest suggested it was time to leave, but as they turned to go, the reporter noticed something. "It was very quick," he wrote later. "Like a falling star, but moved just above the grass. By the time I wheeled around and got my glasses on the spot it had vanished." The description may be quite accurate: some witnesses in the past had described the ghost as nothing more than a shapeless ball of light.

In the early 1980s, several students from the University of

Victoria reported seeing the ghost at its familiar spot, and on another occasion she was reported by two people driving by in a car. The ghost, it seems, has returned to active duty.

Some researchers, however, have been bothered by one or two points about the Golf Course Ghost story. First, it seems strange that she's frequently described as wearing a sheer white wedding dress. It certainly would not have been the outfit she wore to meet her husband that fatal night. Victor and Doris were hardly newlyweds. Also, why she has become so closely associated with young people is difficult to explain. After all, 30-year-old Mrs. Gravlin was no longer a teenager. The fact remains though that the Golf Course Ghost is one of Canada's most sought-after apparitions.

* * * * *

As was mentioned earlier, ghosts seem to have little choice about where they haunt — often the scene of their death or a place of great unhappiness — and are usually not seen very far away from that spot. In the case of this unfortunate lady, it may be that she is bound to the lonely golf course.

Some years ago a young couple rented an old house that they soon discovered was haunted. As is sometimes true in these cases, the couple became quite attached to the presence, even calling him "Henry." (No ghost ever materialized; only strange sounds were heard, while objects seemed to move on their own.) All was fine for a number of years, but the house was built on land zoned for apartments, and the owner eventually made plans to demolish it. The couple had to move out and they were most upset at the thought of leaving Henry. He was almost one of the family.

One day just before they were supposed to move, the couple took two chairs and sat in the laundry room. This seemed to be Henry's favourite room; he was particularly fond of playing with the ironing board. The man explained as best he could that they had to move from the house, and that they had no choice. The woman said they had purchased a house not very

far away — she gave the address —and that Henry was wel-
come to come with them, since *his* house was about to be torn
down, anyway Much to thcir soɪɪow, Henry didn't go with
them. As they said later, their new home was nice, but there
seemed to be something missing.

More Places

It is easy to imagine that ghosts prefer a dusty old house full of cobwebs or isolated places like a golf course, but the evidence suggests that just about any place can be haunted. Here are a few rather unorthodox haunts.

Haunted Highways

While quite common in other parts of the world — Britain, for example, has quite a number of very eerie stretches of road — so-called "haunted highways," are quite rare in Canada. British Columbia, however, has a few such roads. On the highway between Victoria and Sooke on Vancouver Island there is a spot known locally as China Flats.

Some time in the early 1940s an elderly Chinese couple homesteaded a few acres there. One day the woman was suddenly stricken ill and her husband could see she was in immediate need of a doctor. Because he didn't own a car, the farmer made his way to the highway and attempted to hitchhike a ride from a passing vehicle. None of the cars would stop and give the poor man a ride. Finally out of sheer frustration he stepped out into the middle of the highway and began waving his hands. An on-coming car struck and killed him. When authorities arrived at the farm later to break the tragic news to his wife, they found her dead.

Since then, a number of people taking the Sooke Highway have reported that a figure has suddenly darted out from the side of the road. Drivers have had to swerve immediately and jam on the brake to avoid striking the figure. When they have gone back to the spot they have found no one there.

On at least one occasion, the hitchhiker has managed to obtain a ride. A local couple reported that while they were driving along that stretch of highway they were suddenly joined by a ghost in the back seat of their car. While the presence was not visible, both the man and the woman were convinced something had entered the rear seat of their car. What makes the story especially convincing is that at the time of the incident, the couple was not aware of the story of the Chinese hitchhiker.

Another haunted road is a section of the Upper Levels Highway, which connects Vancouver with Horseshoe Bay. A number of motorists have reported that when they reached a stretch of road near Cypress Creek their cars would be suddenly carried along the road by some unknown force. One driver reported an apparition standing on the road, while others claim to have seen a strange red mist hanging just above the highway.

The police and highway authorities claimed the sightings were caused by natural mists, winds and even earthquakes, but Charles Yates, an authority on the history of local Indians, was more thoughtful. He noted that the Cypress Creek area was the site of a big battle between the Squamish and Haida tribes many years before the coming of the white man. One may wonder if it is the spirits of dead warriors haunting that spot.

The Siwash Cemetery

Haunted cemeteries are nothing new, but it is surprising when one graveyard becomes the focus of sudden ghostly activity and then, just as abruptly, all ghostly happenings cease. This was the case during the Christmas holiday season in 1940, when a number of people witnessed a ghost in the vicinity of the little Indian graveyard on Siwash Hill near Courtenay on

Vancouver Island — at a place where the road passed near the cemetery and the shoreline.

What happened during the first appearance is not known, but a week later, on January 2, 1941, the spectre was seen again, this time by logging camp mechanic, Bill Spurrill. While bicycling to work before dawn one morning, Spurrill reported seeing a "white swaying shape" across the road.[1] He brought his bicycle to a halt and watched as the shape began to assume a green glow. As he watched, it took on the outline of a human form, and then began to dissolve into nothingness.

A sceptic about such things, Spurrill ventured the notion that th, ghost was caused by mist spilling over a nearby dyke and picking up the phosphorus in the sea spray. He did not explain how the mist took on human form, nor did his reasoning satisfy everybody. Another morning while again cycling to work in the dark, he found three sailors huddled together at the bottom of the hill, terrified. They had witnessed the spectre and, as far as they were concerned, there was no natural explanation. To ensure that they would not come across it again, the trio made it clear that they weren't moving from that spot until the sun had cleared the horizon.

If Spurrill had been correct, and the ghost had been an illusion, people would probably continue to mistake the mist for something supernatural, but there were no further reports of anything unusual in the vicinity of the cemetery. The haunting stopped as suddenly as it had begun.

The Haunted Nightclub

Vancouver's famous Chinatown district, like other places in this province, has played host to many strange goings-on over the years. The centre of a very active Chinatown haunting was a particularly unlikely spot — a popular nightclub known as the Mandarin Gardens at 98 East Pender Street.

The Mandarin Gardens opened its doors for the first time half way through the 1930s. This was not considered a good time to begin a business, but the owners must have believed that the public needed a place to go to forget the depression which by then had settled in across the entire country. They were right; the nightclub soon became a popular place for an evening of dining and dancing.

The mysterious occurrences began in 1938, shortly after the owner of the building, a man by the name of Chan See Wong, died suddenly at the club, and some people were convinced that the ghost was that of the late landlord. The janitor was apparently the first person to realize something was wrong. While alone in the building during the daylight hours, he heard a disembodied voice. Other staff were also aware of strange incidents. Cups would clatter, bowls would shake, and in the drawers, utensils would rattle against each other, though no one would be in the area when this kitchen cacophony began.

There were also incidents concerning the big floor-waxing machine. Much to the annoyance of the floor cleaner, the plug on the machine would be pulled out of the wall. Then, out of nowhere, the terrified employees would hear a burst of uproarious laughter, as if an unseen someone found the goings-on very funny indeed.

The activities of the ghost angered and frustrated many of the two dozen or so Mandarin Gardens staff, and the new manager, Charlie Nelson, did his best to calm their fears. As far as Nelson was concerned, the ghost was simply a product of overactive imaginations. However, one Saturday morning not long after he had taken the job at the Mandarin Gardens, his opinion about ghosts was to change abruptly.

Nelson was alone in his office working on the bank deposits when he heard something that caused a chill to run up his spine. It was the sound of a male voice, laughing. Not a pleasant sound at all, but a cold, sharp, and under the circumstances, very frightening laugh. He looked up just in time to see a hand in the doorway of the kitchen a few feet away from where he was sitting. The hand itself looked to be perfectly ordinary — except that it was disembodied. It just floated there in mid air.

It was then, Nelson later recalled, that he began believing in ghosts. He quickly fled his office and made his way to the police station which was up the street. ("I didn't run three and a half blocks because I was scared," he admitted later. "Let's just say I was a little nervous.")[2] Once there he explained what had happened and then returned to the nightclub with police constable David Scotland. Together the two men searched the premises. To Nelson's consternation, there was no sign of the disembodied hand. Nor could the two men find anything else out of the ordinary. The ghost had a laugh at the expense of the embarrassed club manager, but Nelson would have the last laugh. In 1952 the building was torn down by order of Vancouver City Council. No one, of course, knows what happened to the Mandarin phantom — the spectre with the bizarre sense of humour was never seen nor heard from again.

The Phantom Dance

Although only a few minutes by boat from the bustling Vancouver Island community of Nanaimo, Valdez Island could be a thousand miles away. The island is an example of a feature quite common in British Columbia: isolated locations which exist virtually in sight of major metropolitan areas.

In the summer of 1961, the well-known syndicated columnist, Jack Scott, and his wife were spending a pleasant summer vacation sailing among the Gulf Islands, the beautiful little islands that dot the sea between southern Vancouver Island and the mainland. The weather was ideal, and the couple's time was, with one exception, their own. The Scotts had planned a rendezvous with another couple, Gordon Graham and his wife, Lou. Graham, who was with the R.C.M.P. detachment at Ganges on Saltspring Island, was a long-time friend of the Scotts.

The Scotts arrived Friday, August 18, at Valdez Spit, on the southern tip of the island. The plan was to spend the weekend fishing. The Grahams weren't expected until the evening, so

Scott and his wife spent the day preparing a camp. The couple selected a location a little north of the spit that seemed ideal. The spot offered good protection for small boats, and just above the high-water mark there was a grassy knoll that angled sharply up to a cliff covered in a thick growth of trees. Here they erected their heavy tent.

It was not until almost sunset that the Grahams arrived. The two couples spent an enjoyable evening sitting around the campfire watching the stars come out. About midnight, the four said goodnight and retired to bed. The fire, which had been built up during the evening, was blazing away.

Some time between two and three in the morning, Scott was awakened by a noise. As he drifted toward consciousness he realized that it was the sound of drums beating out a constant rhythm. Scott lay in his sleeping bag watching the firelight as it was projected on the canvas overhead. Curiously, he felt no fear. His natural reaction was to think that he was dreaming, but he knew he wasn't. Slowly, he rolled over on his stomach and propped himself up by his elbows. "Beyond the glowing embers I could see a great crowd of Indians dancing in the moonlight," Scott wrote later. "There was no sound from them, only the steady, muffled rhythm of drums as they moved gracefully and sinuously in and out of the perimeter of the beach fire."[3]

Scott watched the spectacle for a few minutes without feeling any alarm. He was about to wake his wife to show her the incredible sight, when the policeman stirred and pulled himself out of his sleeping bag to put more wood on the fire. The fantastic dancing images then dissolved. Scott rolled over in his sleeping bag, thinking about the extraordinary display he'd just witnessed. Within minutes he had fallen fast asleep.

Hard-headed newspaper man that he was, Scott was at first reluctant to mention the incident to his wife and friends the next day. Yet the image was so real that he felt compelled to walk along the beach looking for the footprints of the dancers. There should have been hundreds of prints at the place where the Indians had danced the previous night. He, of course, found none. Later, Graham phoned Scott from his office in Ganges. There had been a surprising development to the story. Graham informed him that two boys had found the mummified remains of a young Indian lad on Valdez Island, not far from where the two couples had camped. Also, Graham had spoken to a provincial government anthropologist at Victoria who confirmed that the area north of the spit was a Haida burial ground. "Seems there's a thousand or more Haidas buried all along the beach there, many of them victims of plague or smallpox," Graham told Scott.

The incident continued to bother Scott for some time. It was ten years before the columnist could bring himself to write about what had happened. When he finally did, he called the story "The Night I Began to Believe in Ghosts."

The Macabre Walkway

There was more than one ghost haunting the small apartment building in the Vancouver suburb of Coquitlam. Most were quite gentle presences that would do no more than occasionally let the tenants know they were around, but there was one entity that was not benign like the others: it was truly a terror.

It all started in the summer of 1985, after the owner of the apartment obtained a load of granite slabs for a walkway. One day after they were in place, a tenant, Mrs. Lucille Schneider, turned one of the stones over to discover that they were grave markers. Apparently the walkway was constructed from headstones that had been removed from graves when the Woodlands School for the mentally disabled turned its small cemetery into a park.

After that, "things" suddenly started to happen at the apartment building. The dials on the television sets in various units would constantly be changed while no one was in the room, bedroom lights would turn on and off without human intervention, and mysterious footsteps would be heard to echo over the floors of empty rooms.

The ghosts did not seem to feel restricted to any one unit, but haunted the building as a whole. One particularly active presence was dubbed "Harry." "One day," reported one tenant, "I told a visitor that he would have proof soon enough [that Harry was real]. Then the toaster came on by itself and melted a plastic bread holder." On another occasion when the lights were "acting strange," she suggested that Harry should be invited for tea. "Just then, the heating element under the teapot came on."[4]

Early on in the hauntings, a well-known Abbotsford psychic, Ralph Hurst, investigated Harry's activities in the apartment of Mrs. Schneider. Harry, Hurst concluded, was really a twice-married Scots logger named Albert Johnstone who had been killed some years earlier in a work-related accident. The late Mr. Johnstone was a fun-loving sort of fellow who, according to the psychic, was a little on the lazy side. He certainly wasn't an evil individual, and he was the one responsible for the flicking of the lights and other tricks. Mrs. Schneider felt that there were other presences in the house. At times she would catch the image of a child out of the corner of her eye, but when she turned to face it, it was gone.

However, it was not Mrs. Schneider who was the centre of the most unpleasant manifestations, but another family, the Huttons. It started with the four Hutton children. At various times, they complained about seeing faces pressed against the window of the apartment. On other occasions, in the middle of the night, their beds would suddenly begin to shake. Mrs. Hutton could find no reason for these occurrences.

As far as the tenants of the building were concerned, the 130 little tombstones, which formed the walkway to the road, were the cause of the psychic manifestations. For children living in the building, the stones seemed to hold a macabre fascination. One of the tenants shuddered as she recalled that the local children would turn the stones over to reveal the names of the children whose grave they had marked. Finally the tombstones were taken away, but the ghostly activity didn't stop.

It was not until December of 1986 that incidents seemed to reach a peak. Then Mrs. Hutton encountered a particularly frightening apparition outside her bathroom. "I was coming out of the kitchen and there was this figure standing there — he had a robe with red scribbling on it, but no face." The incident was very upsetting to Mrs. Hutton. "I never believed in this kind of thing — I'm not crazy," she said.[5]

The presence of the monk-like figure was the last straw. "There is no way in God's earth I am staying in this house," Mrs. Hutton affirmed. Then she quickly packed up her family and moved out. Another tenant indicated her family had endured about enough, and threatened also to move out. By then, however, the worst of the psychic phenomena were over and the number of occurrences decreased markedly over the next several months.

Today the ghosts still inhabit the Coquitlam apartment building, long-time resident Mrs. Schneider believes, but they are not nearly as active as they once were.

PART III: HAUNTED PEOPLE

Poltergeists

Poltergeists are known for their bizarre antics. During such disturbances it is common to see dishes, furniture and other household objects suddenly fly through the air and smash against a wall. The term "psychokinesis" (PK) is used by parapsychologists to mean influencing real objects without physical means. Hence, the smashing of a teacup against a wall, if it was the result of poltergeist activity, and not fraud or trickery, would be an example of PK. Although often the prime manifestation of poltergeist activity, PK is not the only kind. Poltergeist hauntings may also include the sound of ghostly footsteps, and even visible spectres.

The life of an individual who is the focus of such activity is often made miserable by the haunting. It is believed that these unfortunate people have no conscious control over the poltergeist; indeed, frequently they are unaware of their key role. The cause of the commotions is unknown, but many researchers now feel it has something to do with the release of pent-up psychic energy. The earliest recorded case of poltergeist activity in British Columbia happened 40 years ago in the little Fraser Valley town of Chilliwack.

The Thing

It became known to the residents of Chilliwack as *The Thing*. There was never anything to be seen, but the noise, the loud racket it made: that was a different question.

Anna Duryba had done well for herself. She had moved to Chilliwack from depression-hit Saskatchewan in 1933, and had worked as a domestic in a number of Chilliwack houses until she could afford to buy a ten-acre chicken ranch about a mile from town. Miss Duryba's house was a four-room cottage, almost new, finished in a then-common imitation brick siding. In May 1951, Miss Duryba's 14-year-old niece, Kathleen, came from Saskatchewan to be her aunt's companion, and several months later, the strange disturbances began at the little farmhouse they shared.

It was the beginning of October when the two women were first aware that something was terribly wrong. It started out as a banging sound on the northeast corner of the house. Even early on, the phenomenon was very loud — one witness described the noise as like a jack hammer striking the corner of the house. In view of the intensity of the disturbance, it seemed logical to assume that the noises were man-made.

At first Miss Duryba was convinced that the noise was created by a prankster, or maybe someone with a grudge against the family. As the disturbances continued though, she concluded that the persistent noisemaker must be motivated by something more than mischief: someone, she felt, was trying to force her to sell her property.

The difficulty was that it was impossible to catch anyone hitting the house. Moreover, the northeast wall was examined by civic authorities and there was no indication of damage. If something had struck the house with the force of a jack hammer, it should have shown on the wall, yet no marks could be found anywhere. The banging began on any of the outside walls of the house at any time of night, and what was more frightening, the banging moved rapidly around the house, more rapidly than was humanly possible. Worse, the dreadful

cacophony now would erupt almost every night. Miss Duryba
was so upset that she began losing weight, and was often unable to sleep. Young Kathleen, too, was becoming increasingly
distraught.

With the help of her uncle, Alec Duryba, who lived on the
neighbouring farm, Anna Duryba set about catching the mysterious person responsible for the terrible incidents. At the height
of the poltergeist activity, Mr. Duryba described the frustration
involved in attempting to catch *The Thing* :

> We run outside when we hear it. Nothing there. Then we
> hear it on the other side of the house and we run around
> there — nothing there either. Sometimes we go in opposite
> directions around the house but we never see anything.[1]

The occurrences seemed designed specifically to madden and
frustrate the Durybas. Indeed, Miss Duryba refused to believe,
even in the face of considerable evidence to the contrary, that
the banging was caused by anything other than pranksters.
Searchlights were brought in, while Mr. Duryba hid in the
bushes with a shotgun. Neighbours, too, armed with rifles, took
turns staking out the perimeter of the house, but the pounding
continued.

On one occasion Mr. Duryba did have an eerie experience.
"We heard it banging one night and I... ran outside and
looked around and couldn't see anything. I turned around and
just then I felt a sort of wind go by me but I couldn't see anything."

There were several theories offered to explain the noises. One
proposed that the thumping was the result of excessive drying
of the ground under the house. British Columbia was experiencing an exceptionally long "Indian summer" and the soil was
parched. The theory dissolved, however, when the fall rains
finally came. The sounds continued even during the November
downpours. Another theory suggested that the phenomenon
was somehow related to electricity. However, the banging
proved just as loud, and equally discomfiting when the power to

the little cottage was turned off.

It was apparent that there was some kind of malevolent intelligence behind the happenings. On at least one occasion *The Thing* seemed to know what the Durybas were asking of it. According to Miss Duryba:

> I heard him once and ran to the window. I yelled 'Go ahead do it again you silly fool.' Right away I heard it again — bang-bang-bang — right under the window. I was standing right there and I could see there was no one outside.

Similarly, Miss Duryba's uncle was standing outside when he challenged *The Thing* to perform. It did. The house shook and the window rattled right beside him but there was nothing to be seen.

The activities of *The Thing* were not restricted to the violent thumping of the walls. It had also thrown rocks at Miss Duryba, her uncle and her niece. By far though, its favourite trick was thumping the walls of the little cottage. Once, a window in the dwelling was broken by the fury of the onslaught.

It was most fortunate for the Durybas that Reverend W. J. T. Clarke, pastor of Chilliwack's St. Thomas Anglican Church was a student of psychical research. At a time when the general public knew little about them, Reverend Clarke had read extensively on the subject of poltergeists. Reverend Clarke visited the Duryba farm, interviewed the victims of the incidents, and talked with authorities involved with the investigation. In the end the minister concluded that the incident was not caused by pranksters, or even an easily explainable natural phenomenon such as electricity. No: according to Reverend Clarke, what happened at the Duryba farm was definitely supernatural.

Although scientific knowledge of poltergeists then was limited by today's standards, the minister quickly recognized that someone living in the Durybas' house was the focal point of the disturbances. The obvious choice would have been Miss Duryba's niece, Kathleen, for it was then believed that the focus for poltergeist disturbances was usually girls who had recently entered puberty.

Near the end of November 1951, Miss Duryba's niece was sent to Vancouver, both to give her a rest from the goings-on at the little chicken ranch, and to see if the incidents would stop once the girl was removed from the scene. While the disturbances decreased, they reappeared briefly on the evening of December 10, when the banging was heard for the last time. This incident, though, might have been a case of someone lending *The Thing* a helping hand; it was the only time during the two months that marks were found on the house.

It is unfortunate that in 1951, most scientists in North America were entirely closed minded when it came to paranormal occurrences, for the Duryba case does appear to offer compelling evidence for the existence of poltergeists. Psychokinetic (PK) activity is often associated with the poltergeist, and in this case it was very strong: strong enough to shake an entire house. The massive blows rendered against the house, which were the prime (although not the only) manifestation of PK, could not have been done easily by Miss Duryba, her niece, or anyone else.

* * * * *

Until fairly recently psychic investigators believed that poltergeist activity was almost always focussed on a young girl around the age of puberty, but according to American parapsychologist William G. Roll, this is not strictly true. Roll, in his study of 92 poltergeist cases with identifiable focal persons from 1612 to 1974, found that 61% were females, 39% males. The figures, however, tend to be somewhat misleading because the earlier data, for whatever reason, significantly favour women. Lately (1950-1974) the data indicate that men are as likely to be focal persons as women.

In 74 cases, where the age of the focal persons was known, it ranged from 8 to 78 years. The average age for focal males was 17 years, and for females, 15 years.

Summer Activity

For Clarence and Verna Walker (not their real names) of
Vancouver, the sudden eruption of poltergeist activity in their
home created a real problem. The Walker family attended a local church which firmly believed that such supernatural activity
was the work of the devil. Both Mr. and Mrs. Walker were very
uncomfortable with the strange goings-on in their home, but it
was impossible to deny what was happening.

The incident began in the summer of 1968. The two older
Walker children Jane, 17, and Keith, 15, had summer jobs,
while the two younger girls, Jill, 12, and Joyce, 10, had been at
camp for two weeks. The house had been uncommonly quiet
while the children were away, but the peace didn't last long.
The two younger children returned home near the end of August and soon Mrs. Walker had to settle the petty squabbles that
always seem to arise between children close to the same age.

One day Mrs. Walker, used to two weeks of peace and quiet,
was annoyed with their constant quarrelling and decided to
separate them for a while in order to give herself a respite.
Joyce was duly sent to weed the flower bed in the front yard
while Jill polished the furniture in the living room. Mrs. Walker
saved the worst job for herself: cleaning the kitchen range. It
was a hot summer day, and the front and back doors of the east
end home were wide open, though there was no breeze to cool
Mrs. Walker as she scrubbed away at the encrusted oven.

Suddenly the woman was aware that the screen door at the
front of the house was rattling. The noise was distinctive, as if
someone grasped the door and shook it. Mrs. Walker assumed
it was a visitor knocking on the door, although she considered it
was strange that the person did not ring the doorbell. She asked
Jill, who was in the dining room, to answer the door. In a few
moments, Jill said there was no one there.

A few minutes later the screen door rattled again. This time
Mrs. Walker went to the door. Nobody was there. Joyce was at
the far end of the yard near the road — it would have been impossible for her to reach the door, rattle the screen and return

to the flower bed before her mother got to the door. Even more mysterious, according to Joyce, no one had come through the front gate. The incident seemed strange to Mrs. Walker, but she thought no more about it and returned to her work. It was only later, when she looked back on the strange occurrences, that she decided that that was the moment everything began.

The next day Jill and Joyce were in the kitchen helping their mother make a batch of cookies. The girls were busily pressing the batter on a cookie sheet while Mrs. Walker was at the sink beginning to wash up the dirty utensils. On a counter, about halfway between where the girls were working and the sink, there was a half-filled carton of eggs. Mrs. Walker had her hands in a sink full of water when she heard a soft, crushing noise. She turned in time to see the contents of one large egg run down the far wall of the kitchen.

Not surprisingly, Mrs. Walker was furious. She angrily demanded to know which girl had thrown the egg. Both, however, denied guilt. Furthermore, each girl also vouched for the innocence of the other (an extremely rare occurrence). According to the girls, the egg had moved out of its carton, and hovered briefly in the air about a foot above the counter, before flying against the wall and shattering. To Mrs. Walker, this story seemed entirely incredible and both girls spent the rest of the afternoon in their room.

When Mr. Walker returned from work that evening Mrs. Walker explained what had happened. He then talked to the girls but their stories remained unchanged, even in the face of losing further privileges. For the Walkers, who placed a very high value on the truth, the idea that one girl, or, more likely, both, could be lying to their parents was most upsetting. But the alternative explanation — that the devil had entered their Christian home — was even worse. Mr. and Mrs. Walker were unable to decide how to deal with the situation.

Two days later Mrs. Walker and her older daughter, Jane, were sitting on a couch in the living room while the younger girls played a board game on the floor. Suddenly, a small bud vase that had been sitting on the fireplace mantel flew across the room, landing on the carpet near the opposite wall. While everyone witnessing the incident attempted to find a rational explanation for what happened, it was obvious that there was no one close enough to throw the vase. Besides, as Jane remarked later, "The vase didn't behave like it was thrown. It seemed to move too slowly — more like it was being carried." [2]

From then on the frequency of disturbances increased. Drinking glasses picked themselves up from the kitchen counter and landed on the floor; a flower vase suddenly turned over while the family looked on. The kitchen light began to flicker on and off. Walker replaced the bulb, and when that didn't work he checked the fuse and the electrical circuit. He couldn't locate the problem.

The Walkers were extremely upset by the goings-on but they refused to believe in the existence of poltergeists. Mrs. Walker, particularly, regarded the entire incident as a shame upon the family. "It was not something mother thought she could mention to our minister," Jane recalled. "In fact none of us were supposed to mention [the poltergeist] to anyone outside our family."

Fortunately, the burst of psychokinetic activity was very short. By the time school had started early the following month, the disturbances had decreased remarkably, and by the end of September, they had stopped completely. While in retrospect it seems that the focal person for the poltergeist activities was either Jill or Joyce, it is not clear which it was. The poltergeist episode was one extraordinary occurrence within what was otherwise quite an ordinary family.

* * * * *

That Special Friend

One of the most interesting facts about the following case is the length of the poltergeist activity. While poltergeists have been reported to be active for as long as six years, most are considerably shorter. The average, as calculated by Dr. Roll, is only five months. (The Chilliwack poltergeist was active only two months; the Walker case lasted only a little more than four weeks.) The case involving Mrs. McIntyre and her son, Jason, went on for three years.

"Ghost I won't buy, but I'm willing to accept psychokinesis," Mrs. Avril McIntyre told a reporter flatly during a 1976 newspaper interview.[3]

Whatever term was applied, some of the occurrences involving Mrs. McIntyre and 3½-year-old Jason were nothing less than extraordinary. At Mrs. McIntyre's North Vancouver condominium, the unusual incidents seemed to centre around young Jason, beginning when the little boy was still a baby. "One night I found him sitting up in bed roaring with laughter, he was completely exhausted."

As Jason grew older the number of psychic experiences increased. There was something else strange as well. Jason developed an imaginary friend he called "Johnny." Of course almost all young children have imaginary friends, but Jason's was somehow different. Johnny seemed a little too close to the real thing for comfort. "For the past couple of years Jason has woken regularly at midnight and talked to Johnny until four a.m.—I've heard a grown man's voice talking to Jason. I just hide under my bed covers — what a terrible mother I must sound, but it's really scary."[4]

Jason provided a very clear description of his friend. Johnny was about six feet two inches in height with fair hair. During a time when the television serial "Daniel Boone" was important in the little boy's life, Jason described his playmate as wearing buckskins. Could it have been Jason imitating the voice of his frontier hero? Not according to Mrs. McIntyre. "There's no way [Jason] could get his voice down that low."[5]

There were other unexplained phenomena that Mrs. McIntyre observed. When Jason was about two, she recalled, "I went to his bedroom one night and found it in chaos. Bedding had been ripped, toys smashed and the legs of his bed had been torn off." Yet astonishingly, before going into Jason's room she had heard no noise at all. The young woman was extremely upset when she saw the boy's room. "I spanked him, but I regret that now," she admitted. "I realize he couldn't have caused that much damage — it takes two adults to lift his bed, let alone break the legs off."[6]

There was other evidence of "Johnny's" presence. A heavy fire door — much too heavy to be moved by a three-year-old — was found standing open. There was simply no explanation for how the door was moved.

Another strange incident involved a swag lamp that was seen to move back and forth while its shade spun around rapidly. On other occasions, pictures on the wall were moved, while a decorative bottle was seen to sail across the room and hit the chesterfield. Another time the blender, which had been hanging on the kitchen wall, detached itself, and flew several feet above the floor before at last obeying the law of gravity. In each of these instances there was no one in a position to have thrown the objects. Also, cupboard doors and drawers in the kitchen would suddenly fly open for no reason.

Mrs. McIntyre and Jason were not the only witnesses to the occurrences. Friends visiting Mrs. McIntyre claimed to have seen several of the psychokinetic incidents, and a neighbour, 15-year-old Christine Foster said she had seen the pictures move and the swag lamp sway to and fro. But there was something more frightening: she had heard weird, growling noises coming from within the house. Christine's mother, Mrs. Eileen Foster, also observed a number of strange episodes, including the moving lamp, but she was unsure whether to ascribe them to a supernatural cause or not. "I can't say yes and I can't say no," she said.[7]

Mrs. Foster also witnessed one of the strangest phenomena in the McIntyre house: the incident of the reappearing water. One day Mrs. Foster was sitting with Mrs. McIntyre and two other friends at the kitchen table when they noticed that a vase of flowers was filled with rather dirty water. What made the situation weird was that the vase contained artificial flowers, which didn't require watering. Mrs. McIntyre simply emptied the vase, but as Mrs. Foster explained, ". . . no sooner had she returned to the table [than] the vase had water inside again." Three times Mrs. McIntyre emptied the vase, and each time it again filled with water.

Naturally, the strange events were upsetting Mrs. McIntyre. She read a number of books on the subject of psychic powers, and even bought a ouija board. The board didn't seem to be a good idea, however. One night the wooden planchette began acting strangely: it started to move on its own all over the board — no one was touching it. By now the young woman was truly frightened and called a local priest for advice. He listened to her story patiently and then advised her to burn the board immediately. As Mrs. McIntyre soon discovered, the task was not easy. "We needed two cans of fuel in the end," Mrs. McIntyre said, "the board just wouldn't burn."

The McIntyre case sparked the interest of a Vancouver clinical psychologist Dr. Lee Pulos and Toronto psychic researchers Dr. George Owen and his wife, Iris. What did the investigators believe was behind the Johnny phenomenon? "It has nothing to do with spirits, nothing to do with the devil," Mrs. Owen concluded. "It seems to be a way in which certain people release emotional tension."[8]

Members of the Burrard Indian band had other ideas about the manifestations at the McIntyre residence. The band chief, John George, believed that the condominium was located on or near an Indian burial ground, and that Johnny was one of his ancestors. The late Chief Dan George was also convinced that the incident was tied to Indian spirits. "You white people have hypnotism and psychic powers — well so do my ancestors," he told a reporter. "My great-grandfather could make fish appear and disappear."[9]

Mrs. Isobel Colbert, the vice-president of the Vancouver Psychic Society, was also sure that the McIntyre case was connected with local Indians. "Indians just don't like white men building on their burial grounds," she said.[10]

Other Personal Ghosts

Poltergeists can be the source of considerable personal distress. No matter how daunting a haunted house may be, the occupants can always move out, but there is no such option available to someone haunted by a personal ghost. If the haunted person moves, the ghost is likely to move right along.

In some cases though, there is nothing malevolent about a personal haunting. It is motivated by a love so great that it is able to reach beyond the grave. The following stories concern the very best of personal ghosts: those that even after death continue to love and care for the living.

Skipper

Frank Layard (not his real name) was six when his parents bought him a German shepherd puppy. The boy called his new friend Skipper, and for the next nine years the two were almost inseparable. "There was no doubt Skipper was my dog," Mr. Layard later recalled. "He was like a shadow. He'd follow me everywhere."[1]

In 1945, when Frank was eleven, he and his parents moved from their home in Vancouver to a cattle ranch a few miles from Kamloops. Both the boy and the dog loved the outdoor life on the ranch. During the summer holidays Frank and Skipper would spend many hours exploring the dry sagebrush-covered hills a few miles behind the ranch.

One of their favourite destinations was a cabin in the hills where an old man known locally as Sandy lived. "To me Sandy with his full white beard seemed as old as the hills. He was what I guess you'd call a hermit: he lived in a little log cabin a long way off the highway, up this narrow dirt road. But he was really a nice old man and... our nearest neighbour."

One year though, Frank didn't spend his summer vacation on the ranch. When he was 15, his father drove the boy to his grandmother's in Vancouver where the teenager was to help paint the elderly lady's house. As usual Skipper, his faithful companion, went along too.

Frank had only been at his grandmother's a couple of days when he was sent to the neighbourhood corner store to buy some groceries. On the way he held his dog by the collar, but when he reached the store he commanded Skipper to stay outside. Skipper, however, was now a ranch dog, and no longer used to the dangers of traffic. He suddenly darted out into the middle of the road where he was struck by a car. Inside the store, Frank heard the sudden squeal of brakes. "Right off, I knew what happened. It was Skipper." Frank ran outside to find his dog dead in the street.

The boy, of course, was heartbroken. "For months after the accident I would get up in the morning and expect to see Skipper there like he always was. Or on other days I'd think it was a good time to take him out for a run. Then suddenly I'd remember what happened and I'd have a sinking feeling in my stomach. And then I would start to cry."

Yet Frank increasingly experienced a feeling that Skipper *was* there. "I'd be lying on my bed and thinking about Skipper... about how much fun we had," Mr. Layard recalled. "And then for some reason I'd just know he was there with me. I'd look down and know he was lying beside my bed."

During the autumn of the year that Skipper died, Frank would go by himself into the hills, yet he never felt quite alone. Sometimes he would suddenly glance off to the side of the trail and catch a glimpse of a familiar sight walking along beside him. When he looked again it was gone.

Winter came early that year. After the first light snowfall of the season, Frank's father asked the boy to take a horse and ride up to make sure Sandy was set for the winter. On his way to Sandy's the boy was aware of the old familiar feeling. Even if he couldn't see the dog, Frank felt Skipper was there beside him. Sandy's cabin overlooked the narrow winding road that crossed the valley. From the distance Frank could see smoke coming out of the chimney, and hoped the old man had seen him coming and put on a fresh pot of coffee. When Frank had almost reached the old shack, Sandy came outside and greeted the boy.

"Where's your dog?" the old man asked.

"What?" Frank said, surprised. Sandy was well aware of what had happened to Skipper.

"I've been watching you and your new dog from the cabin for some time. He looks just like your old one. But where'd he go?"

Frank explained that he didn't have a new dog, but the old man was adamant. He had seen a dog following along beside the boy's horse. On the way home Frank looked at the hoof prints his horse had made on its way to Sandy's cabin. There indeed, beside the tracks in the soft snow was a set of fresh paw prints. Frank had often seen the paw prints Skipper made in the snow and these looked the same. Stranger still, although it was impossible for a creature of that size to disappear without leaving new tracks in the snow, these paw prints appeared to do just that. The marks had come to within about a hundred yards of the cabin and then suddenly ended.

In the spring Frank's parents bought him a German shepherd puppy. Once the new dog was in the house, Frank was never again aware of the presence of his faithful friend, Skipper. "I guess when I got the puppy, my old shepherd felt it was time to go. It was never the same, though. No dog could re- place Skipper."

Someone to Watch Over Me

Between the time when her parents broke up in 1952, and her father remarried, Eva Roy (not her real name) lived in many different foster homes. What should have been the marvellous golden days of childhood are recalled now as only a dreary grey line of passing weeks, months and years. Yet there was one bright spot in her early life: an all-too-brief time she spent with her grandparents in Victoria. Eva particularly adored her grandfather. "After years of feeling that I didn't belong anywhere (knowing I didn't really), he taught me that I was someone special."[2] Thinking back on the few happy summer days of her childhood Eva remembered spending many fascinating hours with him by the ocean near their home. While Eva played he would sit for hours, smoking his pipe on a large boulder.

When Eva was nine, her grandfather grew ill, and it was impossible for the older couple to continue to look after an active little girl. Eva was taken off to another home. In the summer of 1964, when Eva was 14, she was living with her father and step-mother in a small town in the British Columbia interior. Eva was aware that her grandfather was very sick — she had been to Victoria to see him at Easter — but she didn't realize how ill he was. Then early one morning, about three o'clock, she suddenly awoke and found her grandfather standing beside her bed.

Calling her by a pet name he looked down at her and said, "I've got to go now. . . . But I'll be around if you ever need me." And then he was gone.

The next morning Eva's father broke the news to her gently, that her grandfather had passed away in the night. Eva was of course saddened, but her grandfather's early-morning visit had made it clear to her that their parting wouldn't be forever. "I knew he was there. And I knew he was saying good bye. But it didn't seem like a separation."

Eva soon discovered what he had said was true. Whenever there was a crisis in her life, whenever she needed someone to rely upon, he would come. He would sit by her bed and smoke his pipe as he used to do when she was a little girl, and she would tell him her problems. Life continued to be difficult; Eva was often in conflict with her step-mother, but the fact that he was there to give support made the world at least bearable.

However, as she grew older and was more aware that the materialist world refused to accept visitations from ghosts, Eva began to doubt her own experiences. It was not that her grandfather stopped coming; he still did. It was only that Eva began to convince herself that he was no more than a product of her imagination. "I guess I thought he was something I had to comfort me: that somehow I was manifesting him, but he wasn't really there."

Something was to happen to change that. One day when she was about 20, Eva was staying at a house near the University of British Columbia. The period marked a particularly difficult time in her relationship with the man who would later become her husband. "I was really feeling I was at a critical point and I didn't know what to do. I remember thinking, I wish my grandfather would come."

Not long after Eva had prepared for bed she felt the comforting presence of her grandfather. He was there again, sitting by her bed, smoking his pipe and listening to her problems. When she awoke the next morning she felt better, but assumed it had all been a dream.

Then the old lady who owned the house suddenly approached her. "Who did you have in your room last night?" the woman demanded. "I heard voices."

"Maybe I was talking in my sleep or maybe it was the radio," the girl replied lamely.

"No, no," the woman chided "It wasn't the radio. I also smelled pipe smoke."

That night was the last time Eva saw her grandfather. Today, she wants to see him more than ever, but knowing that his visits to her room were more than a product of her imagination has also made her afraid. She wonders if the fear brought about by knowing the truth about after-death survival has prevented him from ever appearing to her again.

A Message from the Grave

The final story of this chapter concerns quite a common phenomenon: the message-bearing crisis apparition. What is particularly interesting about this case, however, is that the message was surprisingly literal.

When it comes to ghosts, it sometimes takes a particular incident to change a sceptic into a believer. This was the case with Andrea Lancaster who literally received a message from the grave. In 1985 she was living with her parents in their Maple Ridge home. It was not a particularly happy time for the family because one of her father's sisters — her Aunt Doris who lived in England — was seriously ill.

One evening Andrea had gone to bed, but had not yet fallen asleep, when she was suddenly aware of a light in her room. At first she thought that it was the reflection of a hall light in her mirror, but as she watched, fascinated, she saw that something was coming into focus. She recognized the scene before her as the cemetery near the town where her aunt lived. There in front of Andrea was the familiar family plot marked out clearly by a border of stones and shaded by an ancient oak tree. Freshly dug earth stood beside a grave. Standing there with the lower part of her body concealed in the open grave was Aunt Doris. Though her aunt had suffered terribly with a debilitating disease, the apparition before Andrea seemed miraculously restored to her previous good health.

As Andrea watched, the figure standing in the grave spoke to her. "Her voice wasn't frail or anything," Andrea recalled later. "It was just as strong as when I'd last heard it."[3]

"I want to go. I'm in so much pain," Aunt Doris said. "But I don't want to leave you or your father." After that the image slowly dissolved. The message had been perfectly clear. While her aunt was reluctant to pass on and leave her loved ones, the time was very, very near.

Three days later Andrea and her family received word from England that her father's sister had died. Aunt Doris could wait no longer.

PART IV: EARLY BRITISH COLUMBIA GHOST STORIES

The Ghost Who Hung a Man and Other Tales

When gold was discovered in the remote Cariboo district of the colony in 1860, thousands of miners trekked into the new goldfield. (In the spring of 1862 alone, an estimated 4,000 miners made the treacherous 400-mile journey between Yale on the Fraser River and Williams Creek, site of the strike.) A number of towns sprang up quite suddenly. Most were hardly more than mining camps, but gradually some of these tent cities took on a kind of permanence. The biggest and most important of the new towns came to be known as Barkerville. Named after the miner, Billy Barker, who had struck it rich at Williams Creek in 1862, Barkerville and the surrounding mining camps grew to reach a population as high as 16,000 by the peak of the rush. As well as saloons, dance halls, hotels, stores, a newspaper and a theatre, Barkerville had its own brew and even its own ghost or two.

The Ghost Who Hung a Man

This story of how Barkerville's famous black barber, Wellington Delaney Moses, named the murderer of a wealthy young man, Morgan Blessing, is not part of the public record. Yet the tale has been around a long time and there are many variations to the story. The first printed version dates back to the turn of the century, but it was probably passed on among the miners of the Cariboo in the best oral tradition long before then.

Not even his friends were sure where Wellington Moses came from originally, but it is known he arrived during the Fraser River gold rush in 1858 and set up a barber shop in Victoria. Moses's business prospered, but with the Cariboo gold rush in full swing, Moses yearned to be a little closer to the action. He quit Victoria and opened a barber shop in Barkerville. Here too Moses prospered. Before long he added a line of women's clothes to his business.

During the extremely frigid Cariboo winters, business in Barkerville slowed, and Moses went to New Westminster to spend the coldest months of the year. It was there that the barber met Morgan Blessing. Blessing was a member of a Boston family who had come from California to seek his fortune at the Cariboo goldfields. In the spring of 1866 the two men decided to go to Barkerville together. Although they had little in common, Blessing and Moses had become quite friendly.

Unlike many who took the rugged Cariboo road, Blessing was well off and, despite Moses's warnings, the Bostonian injudiciously made no secret of this fact. In one saloon along the way Blessing paid for a couple of beer with a $20 bill. Also, he imprudently wore a large scarf pin made from a huge gold nugget. Many of those on the trail marvelled at the pin, which looked like an angel. Blessing was very proud of it, calling it his "guardian angel."

A third man joined Moses and Blessing, an American by the name of James Barry. Unlike the other two men, Barry was down on his luck to the point of being broke. A gambler by trade, the Texan boasted to his new acquaintances that he was going to hit it big in Barkerville.

At a hotel along the trail Blessing arranged for a room while his friends went to the bar. Later, when the angel scarf pin was being shown to some miners, it went missing. Barry claimed that Moses was the last man in the group to have had the object, and Blessing believed him. He begged Moses to return the angel. Many of the hotel's drunken patrons favoured lynching Moses on the spot, but the landlord intervened. Amid hoots and

Barkerville, before the fire of 1868. (COURTESY OF BC ARCHIVES)

jeers from the miners, the barber was ordered to leave the public house, and continued on to Barkerville alone.

Once in Barkerville, Moses resumed business. Not the kind of man to hold a grudge, he looked around town for his former friend but while he saw the gambler, Barry, often enough, there was no sign of Blessing. Barry's luck, Moses noted, seemed to have changed for the better, for now he was wearing fine clothes, and entertaining some of Barkerville's most beautiful ladies. One day Moses stopped the gambler and asked him what had happened to Blessing, but Barry looked away sullenly, and would say only that he didn't know.

Several weeks later, Moses was sitting in his barber shop alone when he was surprised to see Morgan Blessing come in. Usually fastidious about his appearance, Blessing looked terrible. He had many weeks' growth of whiskers on his face and his clothes were rumpled and soiled. The man didn't speak one word to Moses but simply climbed up and sat in the barber chair. Silently, Blessing indicated he wanted his whiskers shaved off. Moses took a hot towel and wrapped it around his face. In seconds, the towel was soaked in blood. Then suddenly the apparition disappeared, leaving Moses staring at the empty chair.

Moses was sure he understood the ghost's message: Morgan Blessing was very dead. Moreover, the barber was convinced he knew who the murderer was. He confided his suspicions to Chief Constable W. H. Fitzgerald, but of course, there was no evidence that a crime had been committed. It was not until September 22, 1866, that Blessing's badly decomposed body was found in a shallow grave at Beaver Pass. There was a single bullet hole in the back of his skull. Barry was tracked down and arrested. There was enough evidence to convict him; he had been foolish enough to give Blessing's angel scarf pin to a local girl.

In July 1867, James Barry was tried before British Columbia's Chief Justice, Matthew Begbie, and found guilty of the murder of Morgan Blessing. One month later, in the neighbouring town of Richfield, Barry took his last walk up the steps of the recently completed gallows; Blessing's murder was avenged.

There is a certain irony to the story, however. In an act typical of his caring nature, Moses spearheaded a public subscription drive so that the unfortunate Blessing was given a proper burial. In the end over a hundred dollars was raised — enough to ensure that Blessing's grave had a neat picket fence and proper marker. Yet when Wellington Delaney Moses died in Barkerville on January 3, 1890, no one in the community did him the equal kindness of securing a marker for his grave, and historians have been unable to trace the resting place of Barkerville's famous barber. Interestingly, the only certainty is that Moses's grave is not in the Barkerville cemetery. That ground was reserved for whites only.

The Tailor's Ghost

Sometimes it's not a good idea to speak of the dead — particularly if the departed soul happens to be listening. One day in the spring of 1873 a Barkerville tailor died and was buried in the local cemetery. Two or three weeks later, Sandy McLinsey, a neighbour of the dead man, invited a friend of his, a man known only as Dickon, over for a chat and to spend the night. Eventually the conversation turned to the death of the tailor. McLinsey never revealed what was said that evening about his neighbour, but when a peculiar noise was suddenly heard in the next room the two men were sure it was the tailor's ghost. Immediately they shivered and the hair stood up on the nape of their necks. That particular sound had an eerie, hollow, dull ring to it — just like the noise of someone's head hitting the floor. *Thump... thump... thump...* The sounds were accompanied by groans and moans.

McLinsey and Dickon looked about the cabin, but no one was there. Next, they looked around outside but they could find nothing to account for the sound. They were quite shaken by the incident and returned to McLinsey's cabin. *Thump... thump... thump....* In a few minutes the noise began again.

The disturbance ceased when they went outside again to investigate. After this pattern continued several times the men decided to go to bed, pull the covers up over themselves, and try and forget what was happening. Once in bed, the two were treated to a chorus of horrible groans. According to McLinsey, they huddled beneath the covers, their hearts racing, waiting for the appearance of a ghost, a bogeyman or maybe even the devil. When nothing materialized they summoned up the courage to search the cabin from top to bottom, but nothing that accounted for the disturbance could be found. When they were finished, the two men looked at each other and then bolted straight for the nearest saloon.

After one or two shots of hot scotch to "restore the equanimity" of their nervous systems, the men elicited the assistance of some of the braver citizens of Barkerville. After offering a bottle of scotch as a bribe, McLinsey and Dickon persuaded two courageous souls to accompany them back to the cabin and witness the ghostly activities for themselves. After they returned, the candle was extinguished while the men made themselves comfortable. However, much to McLinsey's dismay, in the two hours it took to finish the bottle of scotch, nothing happened. To make matters worse, their guests, after making sure the bottle was empty, laughed at them, saying the haunting was only the result of "natural causes."

Now it was obvious that the ghost had played a double trick on them. First, it had frightened both men thoroughly, and then, when word got around, the pair were made to look like fools before the entire town. McLinsey, however, wasn't so much concerned about looking foolish. He was terrified that the tailor's ghost would return permanently to his cabin and haunt him forever.

For the remainder of the night the two men huddled together in the bed. Quivering at the slightest sound, they tried to imagine what the ghost wanted. McLinsey wondered if the tailor might miss his old dog. Maybe, he considered, it would be a good idea to dispatch the poor animal so that it could join its master. Dickon thought for a moment about what his friend had proposed. Then he admitted he didn't consider this was such a good idea, because he couldn't stand the sight of blood. Without Dickon's backing, McLinsey decided to drop the idea, and the dog was not reunited with its master.

The affair had left McLinsey convinced that "haunted" Barkerville was no place to live. "I dinna think yeel see me back in your toon," he wrote in Scots dialect to the editor of the *Cariboo Sentinel*, "until some toonsfolk take out an affidavy... that evera thing is alreicht." [1]

It isn't known whether McLinsey got his affidavit and returned to Barkerville, or whether he moved elsewhere, but the ghost of the tailor, it seems, played only a short engagement at Barkerville. There is no record of anyone hearing that dreadful *thump... thump... thump...* sound again.

* * * * *

When the gold claims began to run out, Barkerville gradually took on the appearance of a ghost town. By the 1950s many of the historic old structures had deteriorated so badly that they were in danger of collapse. In 1958, after pressure from many of the Cariboo district's leading citizens, the British Columbia government agreed to turn the old town into a historic park. The result has been the gradual restoration of many of the buildings to the extent that today Barkerville has become one of this province's leading tourist attractions.

The refurbishing of Barkerville has had one unexpected consequence: tourists and town residents alike have witnessed a number of strange happenings. According to park staff, the most active building is the Theatre Royal on Main Street.

The original Theatre Royal opened in May 1868, but the great Barkerville fire five months later reduced the theatre (and most of the town) to ashes. In 1869 the Royal was rebuilt. However, as the gold began to run out, there were more and more empty seats in the theatre, and in 1872 the manager turned the house lights down for the last time. After a while the building was put to other uses — at one time even filling the unflattering role of town morgue — but time was leaving its mark. By 1937 the old building had become so unsafe that the entire structure was condemned and it was subsequently torn down to make way for a town hall. As part of the Barkerville reconstruction, a new Theatre Royal was built on the site of the old. As it turned out, this theatre has been far more successful than the first one.

Although the theatre is relatively new, Barkerville residents tell many strange tales about it. One particularly interesting story is unfortunately rather fragmentary. A number of years ago an apparition was seen on the Theatre Royal stage: an extra figure in the chorus line of one of the productions. There are no more details, but this scrap of a tale does illustrate what town residents have known for a long time — Barkerville has always been a focus for psychic occurrences.

There are other stories as well. Sometimes in the middle of a performance actors have glanced toward stage left to see an extra person standing in the wings — someone who shouldn't be there. The apparition is that of a man wearing top hat and tails, with a very neatly trimmed moustache. When the startled performer glances again at the same spot, the man has disappeared. Just who this dapper individual was during his lifetime, or why he now appears in the wings of the Theatre Royal is unknown, but he has been seen by a number of performers.

On one occasion during rehearsals, the performers were surprised to hear the music of what they took to be a dulcimer coming through the public-address speakers. This was very strange for the medieval instrument is rarely played today. As those present in the theatre listened intently, the hum of a woman's voice was added to the sound of the instrument. What made the incident so eerie was that a check of the two sound systems revealed that neither one was turned on.

Then there have been strange episodes involving park staff. The security officers who routinely check the fire alarm system below the stage have reported mysterious footsteps treading the boards above them. Such noises have prompted thorough searches of the building, but they have always revealed nothing.

While the theatre is the scene of the most frequent occurrences, psychic manifestations have been experienced elsewhere. Barkerville residents familiar with the old town report that a number of the dilapidated old structures have cold spots, where the temperature drops appreciably for no apparent reason.

Another centre of strange goings-on is Madame Fannie Bendixon's Saloon and boarding-house. On a number of occasions a woman in old-fashioned dress has been seen looking out a second-storey window onto the street. What makes this surprising is that the stairs to the second floor of the Bendixon building collapsed years ago. Without a ladder, which would be obvious from the street, it is impossible for anyone to reach the upstairs floor of Madame Bendixon's.

The White Lady

One of the earliest ghosts to walk in Victoria was the so-called "White Lady." Her haunt was in and around the old Quadra Street Cemetery. Who the mysterious woman was during her lifetime isn't known, but at one time her ghost was a common sight in the vicinity of the graveyard. Many a Victoria resident claimed to have seen her gliding silently between the headstones before suddenly disappearing into the earth. In the following tale, however, the lady seems to have wandered about six blocks from her usual haunt to Langley Alley.

*   *   *   *   *

For the merchants of Victoria, 1861 had been an excellent year. Most of the supplies needed at the Cariboo gold-mining

Quadra Street Cemetery.   (PHOTOGRAPH BY THE AUTHOR)

camps came from the island city, and Victoria wholesalers and retailers alike were prospering. On the last night of the old year it was not surprising that everyone was in a fine mood to usher in the New Year. Shortly after eight o'clock, three celebrants (their names, unfortunately, have been lost to history) decided to take a frequently used shortcut through Langley Alley, not far from the old Boomerang Inn, a favourite drinking establishment in the young city.

The trio had taken only a few steps down the alley when before them, a white shape materialized abruptly out of the shadows. The figure was that of a young woman of about medium height and rather plain in appearance. She seemed quite ordinary, perfectly solid rather than filmy in appearance, but because she was dressed entirely in white, the men took notice. They were struck by the eeriness of the white figure. As the trio watched her they were aware that she didn't step in the normal way, but instead seemed to float along as if she made

Buildings now fill the back lane known as Langley Alley.
(PHOTOGRAPH BY THE AUTHOR)

no contact with the material surface of the alley. The three men were at first stunned by what they had seen. As they stared with their mouths agape, the figure crossed the alley and disappeared into the shadows at the edge.

The lady's ghostly "walk" was not over. Before the men's astonished eyes, the apparition materialized again, and crossed the alley once more — this time in the opposite direction. The trio moved quickly behind the figure and followed her until she disappeared into the deep shadows beside a carpentry shop. What was so frightening was that the figure made absolutely no sound — no one heard footfalls on the pavement or the rustle of a petticoat. The spectre gave no hint that she was aware of the three witnesses.

The incident with the Langley Alley apparition so upset one of the men that he sought out a newspaper reporter and related the story. The man also admitted that this was not the first time he had seen the woman. About eleven o'clock, two nights earlier, he had been walking along the same alley when he saw the same ghostly figure step in front of him. Her hair was very dark and hung loosely over her shoulders, the man explained to the reporter. On this occasion the spectre proceeded silently until she faded away into the blackness near a machine shop. Although at the time the figure had alarmed him greatly, he had decided to say nothing about it, for fear of ridicule. Now that his two friends had also seen the figure, he felt obliged to report what had happened.

When a Victoria paper carried the story, the reporter seemed to feel compelled to offer some kind of explanation. Rather lamely he concluded, ". . . some wag in the vicinity had thrown a sheet over his head and perambulated the alley for the purpose of working on the fears of weak-minded persons."[2] Further, the reporter advised, the police should keep the lane under observation for future visits from the White Lady. The reporter failed to account for the fact that it was not a sheet that the three men had seen, but something that resembled a real person, save for her colour and the gliding motion when she walked.

By 1903 the lady's nocturnal walking (maybe gliding is a better word) had come to an end. As far as is known she was seen no more. Today, the main Victoria post office stands about where the Boomerang Inn was located, and of the original Langley Alley which ran from Yates Street to Chancery Lane, nothing remains.

Beckley Farm

There are a number of different versions of this story, making the facts difficult to determine. Nonetheless, all versions agree on the basic points: Beckley Farm had more than its share of misery. With such an unhappy past, it was not surprising that Victoria residents believed that the house was haunted.

* * * * *

Beckley Farm was established by the Hudson's Bay Company soon after the founding of Fort Victoria in 1843. After the break-up of the original farm in the early 1860s, the Beckley name was apparently applied to a narrow strip of land between Dallas Road and the water, where in the middle 1860s, a Victoria publisher, George Nias, built a farmhouse.

By 1870, British Columbia's gold boom had collapsed and Victoria had fallen on hard times. Nias moved to Australia with his family and Beckley Farm was abandoned. As the house was nearly new and there had been no tragedy connected with it, except possibly for the dashed dreams of George Nias, there was no reason for ghosts.

In 1872 the house took on a new role. In that year the packet ship, *Prince Alfred*, steamed into Victoria harbour *en route* from San Francisco. City residents who were waiting for the arrival of friends and relatives were distressed to see the yellow contagion flag flying at half-mast. There had been an outbreak of smallpox on board the ship. Most of the passengers were disembarked at Macaulay Point where they were put in quarantine in the naval barracks. Those who had already come down with the disease, seven passengers and crew, were taken to Beckley Farm. (The ship's crew, however, was not put in quarantine. The *Prince Alfred* was permitted to continue to Nanaimo.)

The farmhouse had been quickly refurbished for the arrival of those off the *Prince Alfred* but early on there was something unpleasant about the small house — something that seemed to place an added weight on those unfortunate enough to be confined there. One man in fact escaped from Beckley Farm on two separate occasions. After his second escape he was picked up on a Victoria street, much to the distress of city residents who rightly feared the spread of the disease.

On June 23, 1872, a young girl, Bertha Whitney, died from the illness. Several days later the contagion claimed another fatality, this time an unidentified sailor from the *Prince Alfred*. Both victims were buried on Beckley Farm.

After the last patient had left, Beckley Farm again fell to the mercy of the elements and the creatures of the night. Later in 1872, a well-dressed man registered at Victoria's Angel Hotel as P. Lackie (one version of this tale gives his name as P. Locker) from San Francisco. During the several weeks he stayed at the hotel, the man kept to himself, giving no indication as to what his business was, or why he had come to the city. Those who observed him closely, however, believed that something heavy was weighing on his mind.

Only once did the taciturn San Franciscan divulge anything about himself. One day he mentioned to the hotel clerk that he was expecting his wife, who was sailing from England to join him soon, and that he needed suitable accommodations. The clerk, being a practical man, suggested Beckley Farm. After all, it had been recently refurbished, and remained open for the taking. Lackie was much taken with the idea and set about putting the place in order.

The Angel Hotel guests looked forward to the arrival of Mrs. Lackie, so when, early in January 1873, one of the guests was riding on Dallas Road, not far from Beckley Farm, and observed Lackie in the company of an unknown woman, he was naturally intrigued. According to the guest, a young man by the name of Rufus, she was a tall woman with dark hair. As he approached the pair, Rufus was surprised to see the woman suddenly turn and with considerable force, strike Lackie across the face with what might have been a riding stick. This was no light blow, but delivered with considerable force. Not wishing to become involved in what he took to be a domestic quarrel, Rufus rode on.

That evening when Lackie returned to the Angel Hotel for dinner, Rufus noted he had a huge red welt across his cheek. Of the woman, nothing was ever seen again. From that day on Lackie made no mention of his wife, or of his intention to occupy Beckley Farm.

A month later the body of a man dressed in rags was discovered in the Beckley Farm stables, a single bullet having passed through the skull. Several days passed before positive identification was made. Because of the dreadful state of the clothing, many of the guests of the Angel Hotel failed to recognize the body, but eventually it was determined to be Lackie. The San Franciscan had always been a natty dresser; the victim was in tatters.

Because there was no gun by the body, Victoria police concluded it was murder. The truth, however, was revealed several days later. Lackie's body was first discovered by several local Indians who decided that the late San Franciscan had no further need of his expensive wardrobe. They changed clothes with the victim, and then removed the pistol which was lying beside the body. With this information the police concluded that Lackie's death was suicide. It was strongly believed that Lackie had murdered the darkhaired woman in a fit of passion and buried her body somewhere on Beckley Farm. Later, when he was overcome by remorse, he turned his gun on himself.

Now the deserted farmhouse was the site of strange goings-on. At night lights were seen burning in the empty windows. On occasion, people walking along Dallas Road late in the evening reported hearing the ear-piercing scream of a woman. Many people believed that the screams came from the soul of the mysterious woman and this may have been the case, for it was only after the man's suicide that clues to the possible identity of the woman emerged.

The owner of a Victoria boarding-house reported that one of his boarders was missing. A tall, dark-complexioned woman by the name of Gourlay, who claimed to be new to Victoria, had taken a room in his establishment at the beginning of the year. One afternoon she simply went out, never to return. All her belongings, even her personal possessions, were left in the room, and the date of her disappearance was fixed at about the same time as Rufus recalled seeing the pair on Beckley Farm. Less than a year after Lackie's suicide a fire broke out in the farmhouse, and it was completely destroyed. The cause of the fire was never found, but there was more than one Victoria resident who believed that the flames were the only way to expunge the wickedness from the dwelling.

Yet this was still not the end of Beckley Farm's misery (at least according to one version of this tale). About a year after the fire something bizarre occurred. A young woman who had been a patient at Beckley Farm and recovered had subsequently moved to New Westminster. One day she decided to send the dress she had worn as a patient at Beckley to a local dressmaker to be remodelled. Before the job was completed, the dressmaker and several others in her household who had handled the dress came down with smallpox and died. Whether or not the dress was responsible for the outbreak will never be known, but it does seem possible — clothing has long been recognized as a primary source of the spread of smallpox. In Victoria, however, there were undoubtedly many who would have taken a different view — Beckley Farm had finally claimed its last victims.

Victoria and Barkerville were not the only early communities that shared ghostly happenings. The following ghost stories take place in other parts of pioneer British Columbia.

Vancouver: The Haunted Bed

Like most folk narratives, this tale is missing many details. Although we know the story's general location we do not know the names of the principals involved or exactly when it occurred. Still, even if the facts are more than a little fuzzy it is a wonderful story.

Today, almost all the magnificent old houses of Vancouver's West End are gone. In their place, standing like tombstones for block after block, are a myriad of tall, featureless apartment buildings. However, long before one particular house fell to the wrecker's ball, something very unusual occurred there. The incident was so strange that it caused the young couple who owned the house to put it up for sale immediately.

Not long after the turn of the century, a middle-aged couple moved to Vancouver and built a new house in the West End. The pair had been there less than a year when the wife suddenly died. (The woman's death was not unexpected, the husband later explained. She had had a serious heart condition.) Overcome with anguish at this terrible loss, the man quickly sold the house and moved away.

Over the next few years the dwelling changed hands several times until it was bought by a young couple for what they believed was a bargain price. Although they were generally very pleased with their home, there was one difficulty. As the couple later confided to their friends, they felt vaguely uncomfortable in it.

Months went by and the feeling continued to hang over the house. Finally, out of desperation, the couple decided to make major changes. Walls were ripped out and ceilings lowered. The entire house was repainted and new carpets were laid in most of the rooms. Their furniture was sold and new items purchased. By the time they were finished the interior of the house looked entirely different. The master bedroom which had seemed to be at the heart of their discomfiture was gone, replaced by a greatly enlarged drawing-room.

When the renovation was completed, the young owners decided to have a party to celebrate their "new" house. Six or seven couples were invited, and the party went well at first. The drawing-room was comfortable enough; the oppressive feeling seemed to have vanished. Then as the new clock on the mantel counted out eleven, a hush fell over the company.

It wasn't as though anyone saw anything at first. It was simply a feeling, as if the air suddenly became cold as a tomb and as heavy as water. Abruptly conversation stopped and several women openly shivered. All eyes turned to one corner of the room, the area that had until recently been the master bedroom. As they watched, something was beginning to materialize out of the air.

What emerged was a gigantic four-poster bed. The image was so clear that the guests were able to tell that the huge bed was constructed of singularly magnificent rosewood. In the middle of this immense bed was the tiny figure of a woman. As she lay there, her eyes lifted until they were cast upon the blurred shape of a man sitting in an antique chair beside the bed. The shrivelled frame and sunken eyes of the bed's occupant made it apparent that the woman was only a breath away from death, but even as gravely ill as she obviously was, she still conveyed a terrible truth to everyone assembled in the room. As she looked up at the figure in the chair, her eyes were filled with pure terror.

Seconds later the image faded. The young people, naturally, were severely shaken by the incident. That night they took a pledge from their friends never to reveal what had just occurred. A few days later, all the new furniture was quickly sold at auction, and the house was put in the hands of a real estate agent.

For some reason — she was never exactly sure why — one of the guests who had been at the party decided to attend the auction of the couple's furniture, and she noticed something strange. There was the carpet that had been so recently laid in the drawing-room. It was, of course, almost new and in perfect condition, except for four deep crushes in the pile that had been made by something very heavy: something about the size of a large four-poster bed.

Nanaimo: The Axe Murderer

During the early years of this century, H. "Jim" Hawthornthwaite was a prominent politician who served in the provincial legislature. About 1900 Hawthornthwaite shared a house in downtown Nanaimo with Arthur Potts, uncle of the city's long-time magistrate, Lionel Beevor-Potts. Nothing unusual was reported there until one day when Hawthornthwaite was in the living room and his friend was occupied in another room of the house. Suddenly, Potts heard the sound of a scuffle coming from the living room. He rushed in to see his friend standing by the fireplace, and holding a poker in a threatening position.

Hawthornthwaite turned to Potts and told him that he had seen someone in the room with him, an Indian man. The apparition was solid and so life-like that Hawthornthwaite at first thought he was facing a living person. What was so frightening about this intruder was that in his hand he carried a blood-stained axe, and was himself covered in blood.

Apparently Hawthornthwaite picked up a poker to defend himself from what he believed was immediate attack. However, by the time Potts reached the room, the apparition had disappeared. If the ghost was ever seen again there is no record of it, and some time later the house was torn down.

Hawthornthwaite was always very reluctant to discuss the incident. However, a number of years later the MLA was induced to relate the story to the Nanaimo chief of police who had an interest in the subject. The chief listened to the story in silence, and then went on to tell Hawthornthwaite that long before he and Potts had occupied the house, it had been the scene of a particularly grisly crime. An Indian man had murdered his wife there. He had done the terrible deed with an axe and his clothes had been soaked in blood. The MLA's description of what he had seen tallied perfectly with the police report on the murder.

Okanagan Landing: The Sinking Spectre

As often happens with early ghost stories, many of the details of this incident have not survived the years. Just before the turn of the century a certain Mr. Hoare was the engineer on the steamer *Aberdeen*, which plied the waters of Okanagan Lake. Mr. Hoare lived near the settlement of Okanagan Landing, on a road that led past a swamp. One day the engineer befriended a tramp who passed his house, and was kind enough to show the unfortunate man some small hospitality. A little while later the tramp was found dead nearby, apparently under mysterious circumstances.

The next year, on the anniversary of the tramp's visit, Hoare was passing the swamp when he noticed something unusual. It was the spectre of the poor vagabond slowly sinking in the mire. After that, he was disturbed by the sound of a strange hound baying at night around the place where he had watched the ghost sink out of sight. Hoare thereafter refused to stay in his house any longer and moved away. What happened to the sinking spectre was never known.

North Vancouver: The Ghost and Jim Wagner

Several years after Hoare had his difficulty with the ghost of the tramp, another spectre was reported, this time on Grouse Mountain. In the spring of 1903, a shingle-bolt cutter, Jim Wagner, claimed that his cabin on the slopes above the town of North Vancouver was haunted by a particularly abhorrent-looking spirit.

Wagner had been given the use of the cabin when he started work for a local shingle company, Woods and Spicer. There was no indication that the cabin had been the scene of a particularly bloody murder or anything else that may have accounted for the haunting, yet what took place left the rugged pioneer a very frightened man. Wagner saw a disembodied head materialize before him. Demonic looking with fierce fiery eyes, the thing seemed to have no difficulty moving through space. Once Wagner even took a shot at it, but the bullet went right through the apparition and lodged harmlessly in the roof of his cabin.

It was about the last week of April 1903, when Wagner first saw the ghost, and during the next two weeks it appeared in the cabin six or seven times. The incidents so unnerved him that the bolt cutter took to keeping a kerosene lamp on all night. Finally, his nerve failed him completely. He decided it would be better to give up his job than remain there and lose his sanity. Wagner took his belongings and moved from the haunted cabin to the Gulf Islands where, as far as is known, he was never bothered by ghosts again.

It is too easy to dismiss Wagner's story as just another case of cabin fever. Wagner was very definite about what happened while he lived in the cabin, and the occurrences were real enough to cause him to quit his job and move away. Before measles, smallpox, and other white man's diseases wiped out many indigenous people, the north shore of Burrard Inlet had a large native population, and possibly Wagner's cabin was built on an Indian burial ground or near the spot of an ancient tribal battle.

Phantom Lights
and Ghost Ships

Unlike the east coast with its long history of shipwreck and disaster, British Columbia has few phantom ships and spectral sailors. There is a tale of a fisherman who visited his favourite pub in one of the small coastal communities for years after being lost at sea, but details of this haunting are now scarce. There is also the story of a mysterious old sailing ship which visited Vancouver Island around the turn of the century, and another concerning a "phantom" pilot who saved the passengers on board an old ship grounded on a reef up the coast. The events in both of these cases, however, probably concern the real, rather than the supernatural, world. The old ship was likely an old scow, while the mysterious pilot, in this case, turned out to be very much flesh and blood.

There are, nonetheless, a few genuine mysteries haunting the pages of British Columbia's maritime history.

Phantom Lights

Mysterious lights that appear either on the sea or on a headland have long been the stuff of sailors' superstitions the world over, and are sometimes regarded as a bad omen. Such lights are also a part of west coast lore. In one case, however, the phantom light stands not as an omen of the future, but a reminder of the past.

On May 26, 1896, the old Point Ellice Bridge in Victoria collapsed, taking 55 men, women and children — the passengers of an ill-fated streetcar which was crossing the bridge at the time — to a watery death. Since then a mysterious red light has been reported moving along one bank of the Gorge at night, not far from where the terrible calamity occurred. The light is said to move quite slowly, about 18 inches off the ground. What the light means in relation to the tragedy is unknown.

There is also a story about a phantom light on the water somewhere off the eastern coast of Vancouver Island. Not long after the turn of the century, timber cruiser Mose Ireland was working along the coast. About two o'clock in the morning he was out alone in his boat about 75 miles northwest of Sechelt. Ireland suddenly noticed a light pierce the darkness. Then as he watched, "the light took the shape of a woman in a white robe, and it floated over the water to me."[1] Ireland, who described himself as a not overly superstitious man and a teetotaler, was frightened.

When he returned to the logging camp on Read Island, Ireland explained what had happened. Not surprisingly, among the other hard-bitten loggers, Ireland's story was received without much sympathy. They told him flatly, he was off his "reckonin." One night when Ireland was again out in his boat, he saw the light for the second time, but in this case it was different: he had witnesses. In the boat with him were two loggers from Read Island.

It was about two o'clock in the morning and the men were rowing from Read Island to Sechelt, where they would catch a boat to Vancouver. They had reached a point about opposite Sechelt when Ireland noticed a strange cloud of light that seemed to float above the water. The bright light moved on for a while, then it suddenly changed: first sparking and then glowing with a steady white light. Then it disappeared, only to reappear again. Finally it disappeared again, and this time it did not return.

The two men travelling with the timber cruiser were clearly

frightened. Ireland tried to convince them that it was a search-light on a navy ship, but it did not behave like any searchlight the two had ever seen. Moreover, both loggers were well aware that there were no large ships anchored in the area. During the remainder of the trip, Ireland noted, neither man had much to say.

In Ireland's opinion, there was no question as to what the light meant. He was sure it was a harbinger of death or mis-fortune. Each time before the passing of someone close to him, he claimed to see the light. Yet, as frightening as this last inci-dent was, Ireland couldn't help but feel a certain satisfaction in knowing he wasn't the only witness to the phantom light. "I'm an old fellow and I live around alone a lot," he said later, "and people might think it fancy if I hadn't had two witnesses to back me up. It's no lie, so I'm not too ashamed to tell it."

The details of this next haunted light are sketchy at best, but the story concerned a married couple living on one of British Columbia's many small coastal islands (the name of the island has been lost). After the outbreak of the First World War, the man enlisted in the army and was soon sent overseas to battle. When he returned a few years later he had changed greatly. It was almost as though his wife no longer knew him. The war had left its marks, but he had not suffered any physical injury; instead, he was terribly scarred emotionally.

From a man who had left home strong and robust, he was now only a shadow of what he had once been. His fear of the dark was so terrible that he carried a lantern around with him even in the daytime, just in case he might be caught without a light as darkness fell. The man's condition must have put a considerable strain on his wife, and one day without telling anyone where she was going, she simply disappeared. Not knowing what happened to his wife, the man was frantic. He took his lantern and scoured the entire island, but she could not be found. Broken hearted, the ex-soldier soon took his own life.

From time to time after that, passing boats claimed to see a mysterious light moving about the island. As far as sailors on the coastal steamers were concerned, there was no doubt that it was the ghost of the poor ex-soldier searching the little island for his lost love.

The Silent Passengers aboard the *Sea King*

In the disastrous San Francisco earthquake of 1906, many of the brick buildings, which had been constructed without thought to earthquakes, collapsed on top of their hapless occupants and many of the victims were never found. Moreover, a fire started as a result of broken gas lines and most of the business district was destroyed. While the survivors valiantly began rebuilding almost as soon as the ashes cooled, it was years before all the destruction was cleared away.

In the year following the disaster, lumber mills along the Pacific coast were hard pressed to meet the needs of the city. In 1907, the American barque, *Sea King*, arrived in San Francisco, and after discharging her cargo needed to take on ballast. In a city so badly damaged this did not present any problem; a giant steam shovel scooped up a pile of twisted metal and loaded it into the ship's hold. Then the vessel completed an uneventful voyage to Seattle where she was to pick up a cargo of lumber.

The men who supervised the unloading of the *Sea King's* ballast in Seattle, however, were in for a gruesome surprise. Unknown to anyone, the vessel had taken on a complement of silent, grinning passengers in San Francisco. Within the contorted pile of structural steel, dock-side workers discovered the skeletons of many quake victims. It was all too clear what had happened: the massive beams and girders had fallen on top of those caught within the crumbling buildings, crushing them to death.

The unfortunate *Sea King*, no stranger to British Columbia waters, was now considered cursed. Not long after the ship had set sail, strange stories circulated among the crew. In the hold, seamen could hear the ghostly rattle of chains, or, what was undoubtedly worse, the terrible groans of the earthquake victims as they suffered and died within the rubble of the buildings.

It would seem that poetic justice requires a suitable fate for the haunted ship — that she would, like so many other vessels, finish up on the rocks of the Pacific coast—but this was not the case. The remainder of the *Sea King's* career was quite unspectacular and she finished her life on the scrap heap.

The Tragic *Valencia*

If measured only by the number of dead, the wreck of the passenger ship *Valencia* in January 1906 was not British Columbia's worst maritime disaster. When the old paddle steamer *Pacific* had gone down off Cape Flattery over 30 years earlier for example, she took with her almost twice as many victims.

However, if sheer terror is an element in disaster's equation, then the loss of the *Valencia* was more tragic, by far. Unlike the *Pacific*, she did not slip quickly below the waves. Instead, like some prey caught in the clutches of a powerful predator, the ill-fated *Valencia* was mercilessly mauled by the brutal North Pacific. For would-be rescuers, the tragedy was all the more bizarre because it seemed to be played out in slow motion. The long anguish of the doomed ship has left its imprint on the west coast, for over the years, the drama of the *Valencia* has been played out over and over again.

On January 20, 1906, the American Steamship Line vessel *Valencia* weighed anchor in San Francisco harbour and steamed north, bound for Seattle, via Victoria. She carried 94 passengers and a 60-member crew. At a few minutes before midnight on Monday, January 22, the *Valencia* struck a submerged reef at Pachena Bay.

Although the *Valencia* had been moving slowly, the force of the impact caused her to shudder from bow to stern. The ship was now hung up on the rocks and Captain O. M. Johnson ordered the engines reversed. As the vessel pulled back she began to fill rapidly with water. The captain realized there was only

The Valencia.   (COURTESY OF BC ARCHIVES)

one chance to save the ship — to beach her. He ordered full speed ahead, but it was too late. Beneath the waterline, the steamer's hull had been ripped open. The *Valencia* was finished, but what was more tragic, the high seas prevented a successful evacuation, and because the *Valencia* was wedged into the rocks close to shore, the rescue ships were unable to get close enough. They stood by helplessly while the stricken ship was pounded to pieces by the waves.

By clambering higher and higher in the ship's tangled rigging, a few survivors withstood the Pacific's onslaught for almost two days, but in the end almost everyone was claimed by the sea. Of the 154 aboard the stricken vessel only 37 escaped.

It was not long after the rescue ships steamed away from the scene of the tragedy that the first strange occurrence was reported. Carrying some of the survivors, the *City of Topeka* sadly made her way toward Seattle and met another ship, outward bound. The *Topeka* hove to in order to relay the news about the unfortunate *Valencia*. There was very little wind that evening, and as the ship slowed, the thick black smoke from her stack settled lazily over the water.

Suddenly to the horror of all those present, a familiar shape emerged in the bank of curling black cloud. Displayed before them in the shifting wisps of smoke was the ghostly shape of the *Valencia*. Had the doomed ship come to pay those few survivors a final goodbye?

The *Valencia* was not ready to disappear from the waters of the North Pacific. Even years later, seamen sailing along the west coast of Vancouver Island would witness a strange phantom wreck. As they watched, the waves of the North Pacific washed over her decks while spectral figures clung desperately to her rigging. The *Valencia's* terrible death scene had to be repeated over and over. There were other mysteries which related to the doomed ship. During the months that followed the wreck, fishermen along the west coast would report seeing lifeboats moving over the open waters, manned by skeletons. As it turned out these tales had an uncanny resemblance to the truth.

About six months after the *Valencia* tragedy, several Indians were exploring caves in Pachena Bay, not far from where the vessel had been wrecked on the reef, when one of them happened on a lifeboat floating in one of the caves. As the man looked inside he was shocked to see, seated at the oars, a ghastly crew of eight skeletons. Like others in the area this cave was huge — 200 feet long, with a large rock partially blocking the entrance.

To get the boat into the cave, it would have been necessary to lift it over the rock. While the remains were probably those from the *Valencia*, why the occupants had gone to all the trouble of trapping themselves within the cave is a mystery. The tides in the area are very treacherous, and when others attempted to return to the spot the surging water always drove them back. The lifeboat with its grisly passengers has never been recovered.

Afterword:
The Ross Bay Ghost

The ghosts that have been described in the preceding chapters have been otherworldly creatures as far as is known, but the final tale of this collection is about an apparition that doesn't quite measure up. This story takes place in Victoria's old Ross Bay Cemetery — a location that looks as if it should be haunted but which, strangely, has very few ghost stories connected with it.

One Christmas Eve, some time in the 1920s, two girls were cutting through the Ross Bay Cemetery grounds on their way home. It wasn't late, only about seven o'clock, but even in the daytime, the cemetery grounds always seemed rather scary. However, as this was Christmas Eve and there was so much excitement going on at home, the girls had more to talk about than ghosts. They chatted on without noticing where they were.

Suddenly both girls jumped back in fear. From one of the grave plots, they witnessed what seemed to be an apparition rise up. The spectre was white and appeared to glow with its own light. Abruptly, it rose in the air and floated away. The girls, needless to say, were terrified, and they ran screaming toward the street-car stop in front of the cemetery, where a crowd of passengers had just alighted from a trolley. Their story caused considerable commotion, particularly when the street-car conductor also admitted to seeing something white floating through the graveyard.

The occurrence caused a stir in Victoria. Some city residents now refused to go anywhere near the cemetery, while members of the local psychic society maintained a lonely night-time vigil at the spot of the supposed haunting, just in case the spirit decided to pay a return visit. After a while, when nothing further happened, the group tired of the activity, and gave it up, and others forgot their fear of the old cemetery, and again passed by without even a sideways glance.

The incident, however, was not entirely forgotten. Some time later, a group of people, standing in a long queue in front of one of Victoria's major theatres, began to chat amongst themselves. Eventually the discussion turned to ghosts, and one man brought up the story of the Ross Bay incident. Many in the line frankly stated their disbelief in ghosts, and made light of the girls' story. Others were less sure. Finally an elderly man stepped forward and said that the girls had been perfectly cor-

Ross Bay Cemetery. (PHOTOGRAPH BY THE AUTHOR)

rect in their description of what they saw. He knew this for a fact because he was the Ross Bay ghost! He went on to explain what had happened.

At the time of the incident Victoria was suffering through one of the periodic recessions that marked the 1920s. With Christmas coming, and the chance of work remote, the man and his friend had hit on an idea to earn money for the holidays. One day when he had passed through the Ross Bay Cemetery, he had noted that many of the tombstones were looking shabby. As many Victoria residents were in the habit of visiting the graves of loved ones during the Christmas season, he came up with the plan of touching up the faded lettering on the graves with gold paint. All that would be necessary then would be to contact the families of the deceased and, for services rendered, "touch" them up for some cash. (The scheme, incidentally, was a huge success; the pair earned a total of more than $250.)

The pair got a list of stones to retouch, bought some expensive gold leaf paint and went to work. The only trouble was that the work took longer than they imagined, and of course, everything had to be finished by Christmas. On Christmas Eve, armed with a flashlight, paint and brushes, as well as a couple of sheets to prevent the wind from blowing away their expensive gold paint, the men were toiling away. All was proceeding satisfactorily, when suddenly a great gust of wind picked up one of the sheets they were using as a windbreak. One man, still tangled in the other sheet, reached up to grab the first sheet, while his friend turned the light in that direction. As it escaped his grasp, he took off after it, still partially tangled in the second sheet.

The two girls happened to walk by at that moment and saw the sheets illuminated in the beam of the flashlight. The scene must have looked like something straight out of a horror film. For his part, the conductor had looked in the direction of the cemetery just in time to see the sheets blow by.

Footnotes

Introduction

[1] Margaret Murray,"What I believe about Ghosts," in *A Gallery of Ghosts*, ed. Andrew MacKenzie (New York: Taplinger, 1972), p. 20.

[2] D. Scott Rogo, *An Experience of Phantoms* (Toronto: Burns and MacEachern, 1974), p. 25.

Tod House

[1] cited in Alice Tomlinson, *Colonist*, September 23, 1979, Magazine Section, p. 15.

[2] cited in Ron Baird, *News-Herald*, February 13, 1950, p. 18.

[3] J. K. Nesbitt, *News-Herald*, January 25, 1947, p.6.

[4] cited in Baird, p.18.

[5] cited in *Ibid.*

Stately Old Haunts

[1] Personal interview with Archie Miller, March 18, 1989.

[2] Isabel Young, *Colonist*, August 23, 1979, Magazine Section, p. 16.

[3] cited in Robin Skelton and Jean Kozocari, *A Gathering of Ghosts* (Regina: Western Producer Prairie Books, 1989), p. 106.

[4] John Armstrong, *Sun*, October 31, 1987, p. H2.

[5] *British Columbia: Pictorial and Biographical* (Vancouver: S. J. Clarke, 1914), I, 60.

[6] Kim Bolan, *Sun*, October 31, 1986, p. A8.

[7] Armstrong, p. H1.

[8] *Ibid.*

[9] Damian Inwood, *Province*, December 15, 1985, p. 10.

[10] *Ibid.*, p. 3.

[11] cited in Armstrong, p. H1.

[12] cited in G. E. Mortimer, *Colonist*, November 11, 1960, p. 2.

The Williams Street Haunting

[1] *Chilliwack Progress*, May 18, 1966, p. 4.

[2] *Province*, May 30, 1966, p. 19, and following three quotes.

[3] *Colonist*, May 31, 1966, p. 1.

[4] *Sun*, June 3, 1966, p. 15.

[5] *Province*, June 6, 1966, p. 1

[6] *Sun*, June 6, 1966, p. 27.

[7] *Province*, June 9, 1966, p. 21.

[8] *Province*, June 24, 1966, p. 10.

[9] *Province*, October 3, 1972, p. 16.

More Houses

[1] Personal interview with Anne Houseman, March 23, 1989.

[2] Margery Wighton, *Sun*, December 27, 1952, p. 18.

[3] cited in *ibid.*

[4] cited in Ernie Fedoruk, *Times*, October 31, 1969, p. 23.
[5] Telephone interview with Rick Johnston, March 11, 1989.
[6] Shelly Fralic, *Sun*, November 1, 1982, p. A1.
[7] Telephone interview with Jim Dodds, March 12, 1990.
[8] Bill Bachop, *Columbian*, May 1, 1963, p. 1.
[9] Telephone interview with Ron Candy, December 6, 1989.

The Phantom of the Burn Unit
[1] cited in personal interview with Alice Bishop (pseudonym), March 28, 1989.
[2] Personal interview with Denny Conrad, March 28, 1989.
[3] cited in *ibid.*
[4] Bishop.
[5] Conrad.
[6] Bishop.
[7] Conrad.

Haunted Schools
[1] Reby Edmond MacDonald, *Times*, September 3, 1938, Magazine Section, p. 8.
[2] Telephone interview with C. J. Clark, April 19, 1989.
[3] James Guy Payne Audain, *Alex Dunsmuir's Dilemma* (Victoria: Sunnylane, 1964), p. 127.

The Phantom of the Links
[1] Arthur Mayse, *Colonist*, October 31, 1964, p. 13.
[2] Fred Curtin, *Province*, April 9, 1964, p. 23.
[3] Diane Janowski, *Colonist*, May 19, 1968, p. 24, and following three quotes.
[4] cited in Eileen Sonin, *More Canadian Ghosts* (Toronto: Simon and Schuster, 1974), p. 93, and following quote.
[5] Al Forrest, *Times*, June 6, 1978, p. 25.

More Places
[1] *Times*, January 10, 1941, p. 6.
[2] cited in Jack Wasserman, *Sun*, August 6, 1952, p. 10.
[3] Jack Scott, *Sun*, August 28, 1971, p. 5.
[4] Walter Melnyk, *Province*, February 21, 1986, p. 4.
[5] Salim Jiwa, *Sun*, December 9, 1986, p. 3, and following quote.

Poltergeists
[1] Chilliwack *Progress*, November 21, 1951, p. 1, and following two quotes.
[2] Personal interview with Jane Walker (pseudonym), March 29, 1989, and following quote.
[3] Douglas Sagi, *Sun*, December 23, 1976, p. 5, and following quote.
[4] Philip Mills, *Province*, December, 23, 1976, p. 8.
[5] Sagi, p. 2.
[6] Mills, p. 1.
[7] Mills, p. 8, and following two quotes.

[8] Sagi, p. 1.
[9] Mills, p. 8.
[10] *Ibid.*

Other Personal Ghosts
[1] Personal interview with Frank Layard (pseudonym), October 29, 1989, and other quotes in this story.
[2] Personal interview with Eva Roy (pseudonym), March 23, 1989, and other quotes in this story.
[3] Personal interview with Andrea Lancaster, November 15, 1989.

The Ghost Who Hung a Man
[1] Sandy McLinsey, Letter, *Cariboo Sentinel*, May 31, 1873, p. 3.
[2] *British Colonist*, January 1, 1862, n.p.

Phantom Lights and Ghost Ships
[1] *Province*, July 21, 1905, p. 1, and following quote.

Bibliography

BOOKS:

Akrigg, G. P. V. and Helen B. Akrigg. *British Columbia Chronicle, 1847-1871*. Vancouver: Discovery Press, 1977.

Auerbach, Loyd. *ESP, Hauntings and Poltergeists: A Parapsychology Handbook*. New York: Warner Books, 1986.

Brunvand, Jan Harold. *The Vanishing Hitchhiker: American Urban Legends and Their Meanings*. New York: Norton, 1981.

Columbo, John Robert. *Mysterious Canada : Strange Sights, Extraordinary Events, and Peculiar Places*. Toronto: Doubleday, 1988.

Finucane, R. C. *Apparitions of the Dead: A Cultural History of Ghosts*. Buffalo, New York: Prometheus, 1984.

Green, Celia and Charles McCreery. *Apparitions*. London: Hamish, 1975.

Forman, Joan. *Haunted East Anglia*. London: Robert Hale, 1974.

Harris Lorraine. *Barkerville: The Town that Gold Built*. Surrey, British Columbia: Hancock House, 1984.

Hervey, Sheila. *Some Canadian Ghosts*. Toronto: Pocket Books-Simon and Schuster, 1973.

Higgins, D. W. *The Mystic Spring: and other Tales of Western Life*. Toronto: William Briggs, 1904.

———. *The Passing of a Race: and more tales of Western Life*. Toronto: William Briggs, 1905.

Leeds, Morton and Gardner Murphy. *The Paranormal and the Normal: A Historical, Philosophical, and Theoretical Perspective*. Metuchen, New Jersey: Scarecrow Press, 1980.

Lindley, Charles. *Lord Halifax's Ghost Book*. 1936; rpt. London: Fontana-Collins, 1968.

MacKenzie, Andrew. *A Gallery of Ghosts*. New York: Taplinger, 1973.

_____. *Apparitions and Ghosts*. London: Arthur Baker, 1971.
_____. *Hauntings and Apparitions*. London: Heinemann, 1982.
Newell, Gordon R. *SOS North Pacific: Tales of Shipwrecks Off the Washington, British Columbia, and Alaska Coasts*. Portland, Oregon: Binfords and Morton, 1955.
Ormsby, Margaret. *British Columbia: A History*. Toronto: Macmillan, 1958.
Paterson, T. W. *British Columbia Shipwrecks*. Langley, British Columbia: Stagecoach Publishing, 1976.
Rogo, D. Scott. *An Experience of Phantoms*. New York: Taplinger, 1974.
_____. *The Poltergeist Experience*. Markham, Ontario: Penguin Books, 1979.
Scott, Bruce. *"Breakers Ahead!": On the Graveyard of the Pacific*. Victoria: Sono Nis, 1982.
Skelton, Robin and Jean Kozocari. *A Gathering of Ghosts: Hauntings and Exorcisms from the Personal Casebook of Robin Skelton and Jean Kozocari*. Saskatoon: Western Producer Prairie Books, 1989.
Sonin, Eileen. *More Canadian Ghosts*. Toronto: Simon and Schuster (Pocket Books), 1974.
Wilson, Colin. *Poltergeist: A Study in Destructive Haunting*. London: New English Library, 1981.
Wolman, Benjamin B., ed. *Handbook of Parapsychology*. Toronto: Van Nostrand and Reinhold, 1977.

NEWSPAPERS:

Chilliwack Progress
Cariboo Sentinel
New Westminster *Columbian*
Vancouver News-Herald
Vancouver *Province*
Vancouver *Sun*
Victoria *Daily (British) Colonist*
Victoria (Daily) Times
Victoria *Times Colonist*

INTERVIEWS:

Bishop, Alice (pseudonym). Personal interview. March 28, 1989.
Candy, Ron. Telephone interview. December 6, 1989.
Clark, C. J. Telephone interview. April 19, 1989.
Conrad, Denny. Personal interview. March 28, 1989.
Dodds, Jim. Telephone interview. March 12, 1990.
Houseman, Anne. Personal interview. March 23, 1989.
Johnston, Rick. Telephone interview. March 11, 1989.
Lancaster, Andrea. Personal interview. November 15, 1989.
Layard, Frank (pseudonym). Personal interview. October 29, 1989.
Miller, Archie. Personal interview. March 18, 1989.
Roy, Eva. (pseudonym). Personal interview. March 23, 1989.
Walker, Jane (pseudonym). Personal interview. March 29, 1989.

Index